DETROIT & SELECTED POEMS

By the same author:

Rococo, Island Press Co-operative, 2017
Testicle & Tomb, Island Press Co-operative, 2016
Asylum Nerves, New & Selected Poems, Puncher & Wattmann, 2015
Ticket to Ride, Island Press Co-operative
Sky Burials, Island Press Co-operative, 2013
Detroit, Island Press Co-operative, 2012
The Beast Should Comply, Flying Island Books, 2011
Drink from the Animal, Island Press Co-operative, 2010
Skin Theory, Puncher & Wattmann, 2009
Wig Hat On, Island Press Co-operative, 2008
Juggernaut, Island Press Co-operative, 2007
25 poetes australiens, (Editor) Ecrits des Forges, Quebec, 2006
Sugar Hits, Island Press Co-operative, 2006
Voodoo Realities, Island Press Co-operative, 2005
Swan Song, Picaro Press, 2004
Auto One, Vagabond Press, 2002
Bread, Black Pepper, 2000
Black Market, Penguin, 1996
Just Desserts, Island Press Co-operative, 1995
With One Skin Less, Hale & Iremonger, 1994
Travel/Writing (with Ania Walwicz), A & R, 1989
Pell Mell, Black Lightning Press, 1988
Outsider Art in Australia, (Editor) Aspect, 1988
Vehicles (with Anthony Mannix), Island Press, 1985
Squeeze, Island Press, 1985
Swarm, Island Press, 1979
More Bath, Less Water, Red Press, 1978
Hear Me Eating, Makar Press, 1977
Mastication Poems, The Saturday Centre, 1977
Chemical Cart, Island Press, 1977
Foot Falls & Notes, The Saturday Centre, 1976

DETROIT & SELECTED POEMS

Philip Hammial

Sheep Meadow Press
Rhinebeck, New York

Designed and typeset by The Sheep Meadow Press
Distributed by The University Press of New England

Cover image: Philip Hammial, *Mr Toyota*

Library of Congress Cataloging-in-Publication Data

Names: Hammial, Philip, author.
Title: Detroit & selected poems / Philip Hammial.
Other titles: Detroit and selected poems
Description: Rhinebeck, New York : Sheep Meadow Press, 2018.
Identifiers: LCCN 2018016722 | ISBN 9781937679828
Classification: LCC PR9619.3.H295 A6 2018 | DDC 821/.914--dc23
LC record available at https://lccn.loc.gov/2018016722

Published by
Sheep Meadow Press
PO Box 84
Rhinebeck, NY 12572

for Genevieve

CONTENTS

from Detroit (2012)

DETROIT

We are not your enemies
We want to bequeath to you vast and strange domains
Where the flower of mystery offers itself to anyone
   who wishes to pluck it
                              – Guillaume Apollinaire

Mayday

In Bragg Alley I opened the eye of a dead bear
(with a long stick in case he was still alive).
Mayday? No, was truly dead & so I asked
for a roll in the hay of anyone in my audience
of three – a damsel fair, a truck driver square & the Mayor
of Iswhich, the village in which
I was trapped, that truck driver's hand
clutching me by my collar
as he gave me to understand that as
an opener of a bear's eye dead or alive
I was about to be hung (a sky-hook from
a cloud descending) by the scruff of my neck.

Kick Ass

A giver of goulash
in a galosh to boot
I'm ready to root
for your team whatever
it's called – Damsel
Dare or Hem
A Skirt, this dowager's please
whose issue I am, dropped
like a stitch I'm not
a nine
or an eight
or a seven.
I'm one
in a hole, just one
of the girls, kiss curls, a pearl
for swine, a maid with attitude.

Moves

They're making the wrong moves – the waltzing dead.
What they need is a good drenching under
one of those sexy waterfalls where savagery
sweetens into open country without definition although
at the base of that hill there's some narrow gauge tracks
emerging from what was probably a coal mine circa
1840, a pony pulling a small gondola, the contents of which
are unceremoniously dumped in the aisle of a 747
where subdued terrorists are calling for their mothers. One
corpse tumbled down a boarding ramp & another to come
at 3pm if the conditions weren't met, & these guys
expect mercy. Pony boys, set them to pulling
gondolas or, better, no-nonsense mistresses
in buggies. Faster, boys, or get a taste
of this whip. Sounds like fun. Wouldn't mind
some pulling myself. Down some country lane
to the manor house, a dungeon in the cellar where
I'll spend the night if I don't get a move on. Stumblebum,
now you're in for it. Stripped & shackled, & tonight's
the Grand Ball, a coming out for fellows like me. Corseted
in leather, waist like a wasp's, I could have taught them –
the waltzing dead – the right moves.

Birthday Boy

A cinquante sandwich, a chance to French, it's
Lenny's line of course
I know I've used it before & will again, right up
to the very end, those sugar-sweet visions
turning sour as Mayhem gets in synch
with a kookaburra's laugh. All you want
on the mattress without preamble as the flags of the ten
most recently extinguished nations are torn to shreds
by laureates who've never had what it takes
to say what was said, crowding instead
into my coffin as it's lowered
into a hole. Bombs
away! It's a sky burial as subtle
as hourglass sand. Hands up,
I surrender &, yes, it is the cotton pickin' case
that I've blown my chance to French, that sandwich
turning fifty in July. Spiked with candles
I've left it for Lenny.

Prodigal Son

Mother – she's sprouted wings, comes at me with
a butterfly-like flitting that makes me squeamish. I don't
know why, possibly because the soup tureen on the kitchen
table is empty & the seven bibbed slurpers (my relatives?)
are swearing on a stack of Bibles (conveniently placed next
to the tureen) that they'll remember me after I'm dead; well,
easy enough to say but
FOR HOW LONG? Look in the tureen,
says one, probably female in spite
of the moustache, can't you see that the cargo
is precious? No, why would I &, look yourself, it's
empty &, no, I refuse on principle to be a credit to this
or any family, which apparently is construed as a signal
for my bodyguards with their snarling dogs to abandon me,
the cowards, leaving me, wrists & ankles bound, a pole
slipped through, to be carried down a long path
into the heart of a black forest, flitting mother urging
my carers (my relatives?) to hurry: the cage
is ready; the inquisitors are growing impatient.

Correction

Idiot, I've mistaken (for the 3rd time) the morning of men
for the night of animals. Fattened
in a feed lot, my ex Gloria would enjoy watching me squirm,
another self-inflicted humiliation. I just can't
seem to stop. The last time, how embarrassing, my dinner party
contention that puppet sex with friends was okay but not
with foes was howled down by everyone present. And then
they milked me, the bastards, for all I was worth, half a pint
at the most, which my hostess (Gloria's sister) gulped down
with a smirk. So milk
under that bridge & more to come if I don't find a way
to keep my opinions to myself. Wear a gag, always,
only taking it off to stuff my mouth with a few
funeral meats while mares thorn. Mares
thorn? Yes, surely it's a striking image that will lead
the astute reader (albeit, by a twisting path) back
to the opening lines which I'm about to correct: the night
of men for the morning of animals.

Affair

We should concern for this affair. Affair
of there ought to be some in kind who refuse to accept
a stand-in (not the first killing that dumped its government) –
white public lovers who dealt as best they could
with the spellers who encroached upon Madame's overly-
ripe sensibilities & were not in the least bit successful, for,
look, there, a naked someone actualised so close
you can smell her as though
she was dead but in fact is still alive, just back
from a holiday in Egypt, or Senegal, or China (Clarity,
some help here) like one of those debutantes who
extract privilege with impossibly dainty fingers, morsels
tidy, morsels teeming with... Thanksgiving just
around the corner blowing its horn, strutting its turkey,
"When the saints come marching in" it's Madame
who leads them, baton twirling, bobby socks
dream girl, 1954; I wasn't in that marching band, if
only I had been I might not have come to this: my life
as a fetish not what it's cracked up to be, can't just
walk up to someone & ask for a good spanking, call it
one for the road or one for the angels in the fountain who fall
like hail on the replica of my struck-dumb grace temporarily
won when I took the hand of a gentle killer & we slipped
through the gate, eluding the Big Boys, the thugs who guard
the Chocolate Farm, a bouquet in my other hand (how
it came to be there I'll never know) for Madame
who refused to accept it, our affair long over she insisted
with a smile that she'd acquired in Egypt, or Senegal, or
China (Clarity, some help here).

Sartorial

I'll have it – the courage to wear what I kill, it
being difficult if not impossible to say at this point
in the proceedings when I ended up in bed
with the wrong family because my admirers (that
motley crowd) were demanding one of my fly-ups. Molly,
have you seen my wings? Now that I've finally mastered
the art of remembering where I've left my glasses
I keep losing my wings. At least with glasses
I can see to find them, no more groping around
on the floor on my hands & knees. Wrong, as in family?
Wrong. Wrong as in now that I'm up & away (she found
my wings in the oven where I left them to dry) at 30,000 feet
there's a problem: the oxygen masks have dropped
& begun to sway hypnotically, a dozen passengers
in a Voodoo trance dancing ecstatically in the aisles
& the rest engrossed in a past lives therapy session
from which they'll emerge as clean as scrubbed boys
for Sunday school. Me, I'm with the Voodoo mob, ridden,
as we all are, by Mami-Wata, the mermaid who, when
she's finished with me, will leave me with a small token
of her appreciation – the nerve to wear what I kill.

Tabloid

My mother? I'm wearing her as tight as I can, as
I always have in that house of religious purpose. Some
purpose, Death for a laugh when in fact
it's an exercise in cross-dressing taken to a conga line
length, a Golden Mile of would-be starlets scratching & tearing
until they're through to the other side, to: Zenshin
A-rippu kosu (a full-body A-lip course), Yoko shouting
Yam sentence! Yam sentence! while I swallow my pride
& get on with it. Note: when Yoko roars yours
truly a tumble in the hay takes with Betty, full-blooded
American girl, just to get back. Spiteful bastard, O just
to get back I do, I do. What Yoko deserves, her cupboard
far from bare, her rendezvous with the wall-eyed assassin
on the Street of the Unhorsed Imam, her commercial plight
with legs to match, her horde of urine in bedside bottles, her
moth-eaten collection of beaver tails. I'm thinking
of wearing her too.

Please

Skipping Louis rope on fire, his scourge the scourge
of the trompe-l'oeil,
& then there's the unalterable fact that I'm weak
on currency & will remain so,
& in addition: the constant chatter of self-denial that spills
from the mouth of the I'm-a-good-girl-I-don't-break-any-
rules who, from a slightly different perspective (seven
inches to the left), we see as she really is: a hag
with a home-sick complex demanding compensation
from that bastard who trained that fox to make off with
the hen of her intelligence or
the 100kg femme fatale who informs (occupies) every line
on the last page of my collected works that (since
I've foolishly agreed to terms now wholly unacceptable)
issues forth as one more magnificent offering
in a long line that starts with Heinrich (his neck
so popular, he's a Nazi too) & continues with Hans
(who at crawling can best anyone) & on
to Claus who, balanced precariously on a flimsy soapbox,
insists that it was a swan (black of course) that was sent
by his mother to murder him & narrowly escaped, hiding
in the Little Market of the Sacred Heart until the coast
was clear & then a run for it until,
yes, it goes on (but not much longer),
he found himself in that alley (Swan Alley) where the men,
every last one of them, had women's hands, all the better
to heal with, please, rid me of my obsessions, as
above, skipping Louis, etc.

Lamps

If it was up to me I'd recommend a heavy dose
of sacred majority as assembled
to bid us adieu our children watch us leave
like smoking lamps into
a night where if we're lucky Love
won't pounce again. Too fragile now
for those shenanigans although
I'd like to think I could still
do it tough, an old man
with a big stick. But after that *procedure*
last year O tell me where
does the sperm go? It makes
a U-turn, stupid, goes into the bladder, gets
pissed out later. Smoking,
as I said, & it *is*
up to me, that dose offstage almost
within reach.

Digression

Another mess of song.
About? Pain's keening: you
be sick for me & I'll for you, my bishop
to your queen. Queen born
as the bastard daughter of a Gauleiter.
Would you have ever guessed? It's blatantly
obvious, as though written on your forehead

like the tattooed stars on the forehead
of the carnival hand who caught Ralph & I
wrecking his dodgy Tilt-A-Whirl
& gave chase, would have beaten us to a pulp
if he'd caught us, Ralph dead two years ago
at seventy & that roustabout, if he's still alive,
would be at least eighty.

The previous seven lines a digression
with only a tenuous connection
to the first seven – fodder
for a mess of song.

Ward Seven

Who's for ward pride?
If not by the light of a maid's lurks
we're paged by what? Number mad with sane
& the Molly you think so fair is a face
for an apricot fan. All
of her curtsies at once, at once, all
of her curtsies at once.
      In a cup
I thought empty the blood of an owl, for who
has wit enough to keep at bay the hounds
of Henry the Eighth, his double
I'm forced to shave. Bury me not in the lap
of a dog, I said, & he did not listen, in the lap
of a dog & he did not listen.
      In father's piano
with the lid nailed shut, that's where I'll be when Henry's
finished with me while his cooks skim off
a right keen breast (a ripe queen's breast), & so
they should for it seems that glaucoma thugs
are close behind, are close behind
with rags for eyes.
     At most
in trams I trust, a dozen dozing
in a depot, in each the corpse
of a man like me who all too soon was quick
through hospital corridors tangled like baobab roots
on the verge of marrow, on the verge of marrow
those baobab roots.
     If by tooth not nail
I judge a hunt those dogs in the thick
of shamed men will be kicked by him

who's for ward pride; for it was him I'm sure
who left a knife on my kitchen table, to do
what with, a knife on my table
to do what with?
                    Not the wit
to know, not wise like an owl
that left its blood in a cup for a queen
to find, to make of it a broth
to quiet Henry's hounds at large
in tangled roots, in tangled roots
at large.
            And for a finale
we turn to the last page (sane
numbered by mad) where a surly nurse
with ten thumbs is dressing my eyes
with ribbon, an obstreperous rainbow
skipping its maid on the verge of marrow, its maid
on the verge of marrow.

On Rapture

Of the seven things you said to my utter negation
the joy of a toy in approximate conjunction
was the worst. Surely you knew
how deeply I suffered a gargantuan
as I littled my much to shivers & nods
in your presence. It was always
a foregone conclusion that I'd beg
at your feet, my down time blamed
for that rubber duck escapade
that gave me girth
& down to earth & a legacy
of seven things to say to my utter elation.

Snow

Arriving at my opening with a dozen
female devotees in tow Rasputin
pulls out a dagger & slices my pretty pictures
into shreds. Why? What offense? Snow
he expected, good white Russian snow
on everything, on my barns, on my horses
& cows, on my flowers & birds, on my tables
& chairs. And on my pretty pictures
no snow, not one flake of good white Russian snow.

Ex Cathedra

On location where trance folk snag –
a drum machine that scrolls down
to Swamp's End, sky stuff spilt
from the quaffing cup of a funeral lord. Might take years
to sort this mess, one snivelling ambush after another
slowing us down. Do we really
natives spot? – some people so populous, if only
they'd stop fibrillating & build beach bodies we might
have a better world: nine steps
to any distance, nine to any wish come true over terrain
as smooth as sex with an overweight transsexual
on April Fool's Day. Which, bugger, is today. If only
we'd checked our calendar before we left
for that raven-viewing party, those obnoxious
ornithologists with their bird calls that pulled the lame
out of their wheelchairs & sent them dancing
down the aisle for a blessing from a priestess
who insisted, & we quote: "Another inch
in this sealed room & the funeral will break
its only wheel."
          That
was some experience, Candomblé by the feel of it, so
frenzied it makes us want to shout words like poets
with string habits, puppets to manipulate
as to brilliance we come by fits & starts.

Bins

Everything
on sale! So what to say
to these burly girls assaulting bins? What
you can't carry in your cupped hands
leave behind? No way, that's suicidal & might
prove fatal (unlike those previous attention-seeking
failures).
      Leapt
on the count – one – & no time off
for good behaviour. Is it true that a deep plunge
is more effective than a shallow? Yes, obviously. So why
evoke culpability when wives one & three were left high
& dry? – so abundant
their sorrow, so loud their prayers, but would they pay
to hear me print a book? – hallelujahs
on every page, enough voice
for two choirs (if you're going to do daft
do it right): sleights of idiom
that mind harm, those begged comparisons palmed off
as apparitional insinuations that buried
the dead of Haiti with the dead of Togo. What
a mix up! –a scramble for place
as house music for God buffs swells
with bloat. Jesus, just a smidgeon
of decorum, please; I can't take much more
of this uproar, these girls with their celebrity screams
mounting me, a ridden god; if only I was I'd replace
everything that's for sale with everything that's not.

By the Sea

I want it so
the dead are blind. Blind the way
Easter comfort washes a stick-dry corpse, passion
as misplaced as that derailed train (Ann Arbor, MI,
1947) that ended up in a church, in
a school room, in my parent's bedroom, can't
remember which. What's happening
to my memory? My
first dog's name? The
ladder joke?
                    Blind as in
the rage our boss manifests when he can't
find some fool to work for a dollar, his
third world mindset hopelessly irreconcilable
with our first. What
about those boys who were playing cards
on a tomb in the shit-infested seaside cemetery
in Rabat (Morocco) in 1963, they
probably would.
                    Speaking of which: Valery's
Le Cimetiere marin in Sete
that I visited in '60, sitting for an hour or two
under a pine tree wondering if I'd ever have
the what-it-takes to write a cemetery
by the sea poem. Probably not, at seventy-three
I don't like my chances. Which could be why
I want it so that the dead are blind
(& deaf as well, this poem as raucous
as the Arabic of those boys in Rabat).

Keeping Track

Your fourth death? Are you kidding me?
It's only your third. Keeping track, smart
guy? Of course, how could I not forget
your third? – that nightclub fire when,
after it was over, they found those bird masks
in the cloak room, one of them yours? Lap dancing
in a stable, the first (small) horse stumbling,
the last (large) galloping, a Rake's Progress
in increments of straw, the law, for once,
on your side: those machines that fined you with child
could not just sally forth with their supposed
wisdom without your say-so; although
just the threat of a water-boarding
could elicit a loud Yes. Wrung like a rag
it was your second (yes, of course
I remember it, that limp-wristed mincing
for months afterward). From stalking horse to...
With these boots... And how you loved it, looking up,
that ring in her clitoris from which you swung, no net
to catch your fall, your first.

Blind

A black horse, galloping, white eyes (it could be blind)
passes behind a black tree covered with white fungus (it could
be blind), & the rider (there is a rider)
he's black too, black cape, black boots,
black hair, white face, white eyes (he could be blind)
bent low, spurs dug in, & suddenly, with so much galloping,
a switch is thrown
& the tree lights up,
a Christmas tree & in its hanging bulbs – faces,
imprisoned spirits, mouths working, screaming? We see
(we aren't blind) but we hear nothing.

Horse

When I'm with the fat horse
I'm the mother I'd like to be, nipples exposed
to mouths with perfect teeth.

When I'm with the fat horse
I'm a slut kneeling for correction; a session
with the Sturm und Drung gang should see me right.

When I'm with the fat horse
as around a fire my sisters sit & sing
I accept the brand as my due.

When I'm with the fat horse
ankles & wrists lashed to a rack
I snuff a candle with my lips.

When I'm with the fat horse
I'm not having sex. The sound that you hear is the *squelch*
of the rubber wheels of electric wheelchairs on a wood floor.

When I'm with the fat horse
there's too much sap in my face, they say, that
it's much too moist & take to it with rags.

When I'm with the thin horse
there's a bridle & steerage
& a moonlit path.

Lovers

If I had a penny for every pony I've ridden
I'd have a nickel, enough to pay
for one of Sylvia's sex assessments
that would speak not of fissures

& dubious genealogies but of clout
& ecstasy. Pot-bellied & prostate-challenged,
Sylvia reckons I'm flypaper
for the over-60s & rid of the pot

I'd have the 50s too. But,
hang on, isn't a question
being begged here – how many women

can fit in a sonnet? Only one
by the look of it,
the above-mentioned Sylvia.

Guerilla Warfare

Is that bridal veil the real deal? Another
dog? I'm already carrying five. So livid
when you let go, why? With string to bind
you have a law to use. But not before

I consult my Dictionary of Biblical Names. Call you
one of them, whatever fits. That fluttering noise,
flags or skin, & if the latter whose? Claim
this victim as your own (before

someone else does). There could
be money involved. We'd better opt
for the real man option in the same way
that a truck's exhaust brakes on a downhill run

feed a church on Sunday morning, the Right
Reverend Jessie Sykes making his debut
as prime-time honey, his stuff sticking
on us like I was stuck on Barbara Wysong

in the summer of '57. Or was it '58? At 68
my memory is a hole in one. The big ones
always get away. Snatch & run: ever feel
that you've been *galloped*? I have, years ago,

long before the Brethren voted *No* on the Burn
Baby Burn referendum: All the fun
out of it, Mick & Mike up
on murder one. And Mad makes three.

Kiss & Tell

Such glass as a shoemaker minds
as a churl in a tower proposes
impeachments, so easy to shush
that witnessing you promised,

that make it up as we move our
mothers up a notch or two to step
to see to the screams of a sweeping girl
in a harrowing box

that harrowing her
the last I saw of the pumpkin prince
he was cadging femmes with Capital
as pernicious as penury, unspecified

as to which fib would fetch
the maid to the ball at St. Eustache
where Santo Bam & Bormann's son
are sure to kiss & tell.

Friend

of an evening, you bring a two-toothed charm to share
    with me?
With you I always feel mustered, why so?
Having disembarked once, twice, thrice, why
        must we a fourth?
Rotterdam, Mombasa, Odessa – any port in a storm
    except (because of wives there) Gdansk, Haiphong,
        Caracas.
Having fed at the trough of daily miracle, if it (Love)
           is about the physics of efflorescence I'm not
                in the least interested.
Not the girl your mother was, dare we hope
                for bang-bang sex?
Often (twice weekly) I wonder what makes a spirit sigh.
As of now (4/10/10) there is a watching involved
        for the one who to us would a mouth gift.
Yes, not to worry, you'll have your season
                  & I'll mine.
This poem to lovers everywhere dedicated.

East of Eden

If the coast is clear
we'll bother all the way, fifty miles
of tough dove until we're back
at the dying part. As
we were before? Not
with that scent on your fingers, you
bastard. Whose is it? What innocent
undone? If only
we could sick no more, Doctor Jesus
with some healing, scent
on his fingers too. I wonder could we skip
the accusation? What to do
with our run-down prize is what
I want to know (have for years been
scarcely in the know, ever since
that sky scaffold fell, dead men down they *do*
tell lies). Their truth (can you hear it?)
in my keeping who can lie with the best, that's
me: Jack of Wallace fame who if he could
would slip past these whispering shades
of whoredom, but not to be: beaten back
by a vision stick, you who wield it if only
you could see your way to some Mary not contrary
it would to me be a great relief; that coast made clear
we could bother all the way.

Emilio

When Emilio presented me with no alternative
but to live a *life exemplum* I sought refuge
in the bats that boys do, so convinced that so certain
of its sight is each animal that something could/had
to be done about that boy dragging that cat
to school, a rope around its scrawny neck, & did, found
a hose for a flush, a deck cleared, a sailor expelled
from a breech (a cat cut loose but too late). And there,
unbreeched, he, Emilio, found me & would
stay on my case until my fours were summed
on a touch screen "What's so ship-at-sea
about me?" I foolishly asked, an envy in a throat
he reckoned with by pointing out
that, yes, although I'd sailed
to world's center what would happen
if I didn't sing? A buy-back, my life,
like a gun? Or, worse: Pull it tight, make
it hurt until what's left is pulp, a fiction embellished
with canned laughter? "That measly one,
is it really me?" It was, & he could smell it, the stench
of my fear. "It's not a rant, this poem, just because
you say so," I sobbed, crawling on all fours toward
what seemed like a mother figure but, as it turned out,
wasn't. "And in the next life I'll do defiance
with a bat. Just wait & see if I don't."

Schroeder's Cat

What's the deal with Denis when
Bad Girl walks the fat? Don't know. Maybe make
the dog tender, maybe grease the rickshaws
that permeate our twilight years, traffic control
not an option with these floating coffins (another
raging flood) broadcasting terror like unlicensed
offshore stations, song adrift inciting Denis
to God knows what act of effervescence, maybe carve
his initials in the mirror-like surface of the Louis XV
escritoire where he sits & broods on what to do: cane trifles
or find a holding garment (wire cage)
for an aging body, stalkers welcome
if they come with elixirs, anything to cop
some shriving stuff to wear like shrouds, life jackets
for the over eighties was it worth that paddle
up that raging creek? – one drop of which
worth as much as a cup of embalming fluid
from Anubis' fabled beaker who knew – Anubis –
the implication of a honeyed snare, the use
of usury: Pittance, Pith & Pity exaggerated
in the public interest that happens
to be Denis' as well he'll make
the dog tender when Bad Girl kills the cat.

Sound

Should I in doubt decry a tune, its
abject failure to extract a boon? Or perhaps
all that's lacking is an opportunity for congratulation, a
Well Done to the one who finally managed to debunk
the animal show.
                How pink
is the sound of spite? Should I keep silent
when you stick? If only you'd seen the page
with my word you'd happily agree
to carry the books I write. You'd be delighted
with their finger-snaps, their eye-opening
approbations. Of that I'm sure. And thus exonerated
I'd not be, as now, the victim (sometimes
willing) of a hard felt stranger, his neck
a dirty turkey one. Of course I could settle
for just a brown sound as, for example, the pitter-
patter of dirt as it lands on a coffin's lid.
                           If she
was my mother by John who is my father
by Tom? – surely not that go-between
on that apparently endless airport belt? Judging
by the parboiled communions he leaves
on my table between flights it can't be. No
father of mine would ever serve up such
charismatic mush. Or would he? And, for
that matter, would I know a boon if one was placed
before me, a bib tied round, a spoon
stuck in my fist, its clink against the bowl
a green sound? Green? – could green be the color
that my father used to debunk the animal show?

Now

Now we hear the word of How
to coerce: grab someone
& squeeze. Yes, done.
But why the cooing? Why not strangulation?
It too has a legitimate claim on a life
that some, less worthy than others, might wear
like contemporary usage. But one
at a time. What's the rush? Best
to wear slowly as one who teaches
an apprentice how to slay gently
every man who could begin a day
of God bless while he tows the Glory Wagon
from past to Now, past Thomas
who rows & Loma who crows
how sweet she'd like to cop it
from the winners of the world, their biplane
roaring overhead, dropping bombs, correction:
a feather that flutters harmlessly down, but Dolly
says Sorry anyway & Thomas says Mire
& Loma Desire (regrets unacceptable to Dot
who picks the tune; so godly strange, this,
as the pipe is carefully placed between
the Wizard's puckered lips while under him
wheels turn & turn; it can't be helped
who won't help themselves): I'm not
who I am, this kneeling my submission
to the hooded monks who now arrive
with staves that on a floor of wood they beat
& beat & beat to no avail. The one with wings
has fallen dead. He will not rise.

Con/Charles

For you we fix.
For you we tell you pack of lies
about your own exception, wolf
at dog's breakfast.

Are you bus or train?
Or part & parcel of automobile?
Me, when I'm dog I'm there
to kiss the feet. Talk of which, what
do I do with this little father
who follows me?

You do a big smile as by
his peril which is red
all the way up to give the lie
to what's been put about – that
his papa is a grab.

No gravy on my chin.
Stare me down if you think you can.
I'll simply elect to ratify.
I'll recall to myself as to a king
what my kingdom was
& again will be.

But weather's all wrong, too wet
to chase women what
I can't have: never again to walk
out under blue sky with blue girl.
For me too late.
For me no fix.

Titanic

Skin tearing like paper as a dozen dolphins
tumble down the grand staircase
into the ballroom. Let's face it, folks,
the dance is over & the lifeboats
won't lower (a mixed metaphor
of tangled ropes & pulleys).
                              The
drowned, their faces pressed up against
thin ice as though against the window
of a sumptuous brothel in Beirut circa
the 50s, cool tiles, warm tapestries, ornate
lion-footed furniture, what
do they want now? They've already had
a better death than I'll ever have.
                              Drag
that life-raft back into that mausoleum
& leave it there while the smoking tycoon
gets his just desserts, his fortune lost
like a smoking gun, an exhausted conceit
to be sure, but it's working; it's
making it (modern life, whatever that is)
almost bearable as though the silent film
I've been watching is accompanied
by a ragtime piano, just
what the doctor ordered, those dolphins
reviving, beginning to wallow
in the old fashioned imagery I've pulled
from a hat. Forget the post-modernist
claptrap; this one's a winner.

Belle Epoch

Pushing ahead with my father's cane
  I'm almost as fast as a true Carioca.
He wants me to remember, to describe in detail
    all of the shoes he's worn.
I'd like to say I'm flush, royal,
   but that would be a lie.
Have we really learned usage? I don't think so.
If only in that overwhelming pull-apart:
   there was a hint of Transgression.
Once anointed, no increase is possible.
Relinquished: our fascination with extravagance.
The intention stretches.
Gaze worn thin, I make airplane.
Ask for a fountain's best.
She came to me with her strings tied.
Was that her most loquacious voice?
Is Lola equipped for homage? Is Lucy?
How they love it: rubberneck fun
    on a spangled night.
Those who signify are too close.
Are these we the people?
In the practice of small theirs is a lunch story.
You can find them on any rag map.
O Lord, find a place for my knees & elbows.
Lord, please feel the dance of me.
What a handful of face!
You're messin' with my scarcity.
Your turn at the salvation wheel.
Make way for the holiness to come.

Escape

Shit for brains, we rock
around the clock, we mock
their fisting as two by two we're marched

in for a feed potatoes & carrots & cabbage & pork
& grootes & glams & maybe & if
we don't shut up they'll trice us

with ilk, with mince & cash express,
with a spoon-fed belief that who beasts
best is our better, who swallows a gaffe

gets our vote for a quote: "Deb's best
at pant swell." Remember
Digger O'Dell? How for a notion

he rang a bell? As hard by half
we petered out. As bards in jackets
of a chemical nature we slid down ropes of merry.

Gang Star

This true account of the savage attack
on Barnabus Pye begins with a little cooking boy posed
with hands on hips he's
trying a leg with no success because
his other side refuses speech. I could
& will liken this failure to a crisis provoked
by my internment in Athens State
(hospital) where I was sent
for Energy Equivocation, to rest
my masculine, that droll flesh
at the Cafe Royal the seed
of my downfall. There for an hour
& no hand touched my thigh presumably because
the cooking boy was driving the touchers away
with a spatula, giving the lie
to the lay of my land, hence my attack
on Barnabus Pye.

Bravo

Sitting in this chair – no feel nothing
& the furthering of it.
                              Did I garner
while I could? Did I detect
a mince? Was I convinced
by the ribbons of the boy? No
& no & no.
                  Because market
was the problem. Also,
that obese man with the poodle
who seems glued to something.

If only I could work out to what...
In any case, if that's him
these are his words: "It's my turn
to hunger you
publically." A right pretty speech
if I say so myself, & I do, & as
for the boy: If I took his ribbon
he'd no feel nothing.

Nights of the Red Feather

On the 6th night of the red feather enter Michael Hand.
How credible his arrival?
How seriously do we take his threat to hang himself
                in the doorway where Nerval did same?
With whom (Nerval) it was either concoction (rope
           plus neck) or collaboration (rope with neck),
probably the former (concoction). Con, yes, but of sorrow
let's do away with now. I say: let no gallant leap
                            to his rescue.
I say: no quarter to those with scurrilous effect.
I say: his turn come now – on the 7th night
of the red feather exit Michael Hand.

Effluent

Sewer gush. Please,
not another radio voice from the roaring 20s – message
received/messenger shot. Best regress
to Default Mode & get a life
before the Dow falls
again, an all-time low, nothing
for a rainy day, Ginger & Fred
hoofing it in a parking lot of burned-out hulks. That
4-door Packard, or what's left of it, wasn't that
Abe Bernstein's, late of the Purple Gang? Speakeasy
nights: you don't get in
if you don't know the password. *Hush.*

Chapter & Verse

For the sake of an *Aleikum*
all of us are *Arias* to please
an imam who's come to take
his rightful place in the sentence being written

as we stand on Qutab Street with Saaqib stopping strollers
with the message that he & he alone must give: that
there's only one thing to get straight – that this poem's
about a bath, so please dissuade yourself of the notion

that it's about a sex divan in Faizabad
where, with Allah's help, we'll soon
be musing on Paradise while cobras
come close enough to spit, but of course

they won't for blessed are the righteous with whom
we're on good terms if not among
their number yet, only waiting
for a clearance from on high, the green light

to click on & hope that in it Saaqib's
not had a hand, his perfect
for stopping strollers but far too glad
for matters as lofty as this that in the context

of a bath might seriously consider human
blood but, no stomach for real violence, settles
on goat, a halal butcher stepping in
to take his place in the sentence being written.

A Lesson

Another urinary episode, yours truly one of thousands
who, in the dead of night, will call out for a bedpan. Nurse,
quick, my life (admittedly antique) is snared by grief, is
culled from some confusion as to where I am. And
when. And, most to the point, why. But as always
she arrives too late, too busy chatting
with the sound effects man. *Your rolls of thunder*
aren't authentic. They need more crack, more Zeus
with a whip.
            Butch favorites
on the mark, get set, go... their divine anatomies
set adrift, so slow; is jelly roll
all they know?
                That every shoe
is worn by someone is a fact
that I know. And ditto glove: *Take that,*
& that. Fifty slaps
by my count, & more to come, more cheek
to turn, a lesson apparently
that I need to learn as I float merrily (Marry me!)
down a river of my own creation, another
  urinary episode.

Chambers

Hospital bed merry-go-round
changes   suddenly   with no warning   to
hospital bed carousel.

The face, yes, by all means, paint it
red, white, blue, but, no, not
a study in brown – a cancer throat.

The captions are in English, the paint
                                        in Dutch

Bodies on their backs, on each stomach, in
                                   red lipstick, huge lips.

A reclining nude a la Goya, Manet... Look
closely; it's a skinny old man, rope
veins, parchment skin.

Above bed pet lamps? Why? Can't read by.

Where the bed was: a display case, surgical
                                   instruments circa 1850.

Crystal organs – heart, lungs, liver, stomach, bladder...
drop them, one by one, into
a metal bucket. Listen.

Ward 10: unmade beds, crow footprints
                                   across sheets.

In this one: a row of toilet cubicles, locks clicking
                                   open/shut.

The angels (cowering in corners)
                    are cross-dressed – XXX.

He lived here for ten years – the enfant Napoleon.

Through this one – clanging all night - Tram Line A runs.

Musical beds: a brain tumour, operable;
you could have done better, or worse.

Peek-a-boo: now you see it, now you don't –
                    the face of Death.

And Furthermore

for Alan Sisley

since there aren't any postcards in this hospital
I can't send my friends pictures of:
   my swollen testicle (left),
   my infected bladder,
   my pneumonia,
   my mild heart attack.
Red alert: another nurse coming to collect
more unmentionables such as:
   blood,
   urine,
   sputum,
   faeces.
Yesterday afternoon Alan stopped by
for an hour chat about art, in my case:
   the art of gritting your teeth when you piss
                       (because it burns),
   the art of squeezing out one small marble
                       (because I'm constipated),
   the art of not vomiting after eating
                       (because I'm nauseous)
and, by the way, before I forget, there's the matter
of my art show at Orange Regional, titles & prices
to sort out, etc. It's a survey show not,
as I keep saying, a retrospective. Apparently
a retrospective is what you have after you're dead
which, in moments of self-pity, I feel
I might soon be. Anyway,
survey or retro, the head doctor assures me
that I can go to my opening
in a wheelchair, a thin grey ghost
packed to the gills with excrement.

Institutional

Another death role
or should it be scroll? Anyway,
here you are hamming it up
on a two-fisted radio
with a gut-bucket voice articulating
a topic close to your heart: on air
protocol, the short & long of how
to get in a bind with deft listeners
of immaculate truths & come out
not only whole but refreshed. First,
with respect to the TTT – Twice
Told Tale – leave something out, such as
the medication or the missing needle
in the haystack that you found
& wouldn't give back until the appointed hour
which was never, never, never in
a million years of cold-blooded indifference
to the fate of those screaming fools trapped
on the Sky Wheel as it began to spin
faster & faster, out of control, a whirlpool
in a river of light, Thy will be done
on earth etc. Second, know simply
when to shut up, that big mouth of yours
open like a shell, Venus about to say something
to her thousands of admirers approaching
in skiffs, canoes, kayaks, rowboats, even a gunboat
or two, sailors ready with grappling hooks, but
she doesn't; she just smiles beatifically, an example
you'd do well to follow, i.e., turn
that stupid radio off.

Countdown

In the wings, my number
to be called: thirty. After eating
my father played with a train. That electricity
had the odor of sanctity from which
I've yet to recover. After the war there were soldiers
on the running boards of my uncle's
'38 Dodge. Was one of them Walter
who would later learn to waltz, the hand
of my mother won thereby? When
it came to health it was the sum of the luggage
I carried. Each year was a receptacle, a primary
moral in each. The nuisance was always
in a shop window. A rich amigo
proposed a thaw. Summer: a test
too strenuous. Which meant that twenty
fell short, the long of it
literature, a trade in lies. For which I must
apologize again. And again. And again. As again
it would seem that there's bread to be had. To
break. To knock some door she had me
to some shrink where down to ten & I'm still
HUGE to her concern. Pills,
she said, would surely help, a cure
I can take but will leave as I'm not & never will be
a miracle fan. And about the Bulgarians
who hide in the slums of Cairo
I have nothing to say.

Blowing

Such maze of happenstance
where you must blow, your wind
a bag brought to bear on a would-
be erotically-primed rabbit foot rendezvous
that seems to suggest that you'll always be met
at airports no matter where or when but
it never happens, those slabs
of fear, those terminal threats
from the sidle-up clan, bit players
with a philosophy of try
anything once – electro shock therapy? –
just for a laugh it's clearly Schizophrenia 295.4:
Schizophreniform, Persecutory subtype
on the DSM-IV Code, although
I'm inclined to go with Nashe – 6000 devils
in the right ear, 5000 in the left, dumped
goods, a field day for the ear merchants, result:
Hotch-potching Scripture again, don't say
you weren't warned, is why
you're still in the maze blowing.

Shame's Parabola

After Lawrence told (for the seventh time)
his lighthouse story Guillaume, Max & I compared
our dreams of Penelope's perfect feet, yours truly
the only one game enough to describe how delicious
they were (taste in a dream?), hence the appellation
MR SHAMELESS on the T-shirt I'm threatening to wear
to Penelope's party tonight.
Is Annabelle going? – the peculiar tension in her life
not arising from nervous impatience but from
the discrepancy between the infinitely modulated surface
of her personality & the still, unmovable profundity
of her soul. What a mouthful!
I'm resisting, I'm trying not to seize her so ardently
that she collapses as though a small but significant
portion of the thread that makes up her life
has been snipped off like a beam of light
abruptly severed by an electricity failure, ships
crashing in the night. You fool,
Annabelle has overheard the nonsense
you've been spouting like a whale up for air.
She's on the phone to Penelope. The party's off.

Touching Miss Moore

There's no amount of what to see.
One neighbour (only one?) is inclined for a lynch.
If trousers change so must skirts.
Talk smut while I rustle.

His main name's Alice.
He's the stuff of legend.
Let's vote for a house lust.
That's one deviant mother.

Another Miss Moore? – that makes three.
Which one famously said nothing?
Me, I'm here for Alice.

Follow from bedroom to forest.
Hunter stumbles, gun goes off.
Death that cozy you couldn't wait for.

Trance

Get in a trance & get
myself back, flush, honey
where it should be, every corner
round & bright, yes.
     Cowboys
on the floor of much concern, only
too ready to substitute their rough face
for my fine, too ready to touch some fool's
deep devotion (read delusion), not
my cup of tea.
    From whom, cowboys,
I'll stay an inch shy that any
of my life for any occasion be as
sugar in myself only; for what am I
if I'm not mine? – that story
I've worked years on just to give away
to some floor boys? No.
      Now
it's coming, soon flush, honey
where it should be, every corner
round & bright.

Meringue

Ok, so I admit I'm living in a big window making noises
like God. And you, you throw a stone. Crash! All this
broken glass shouldn't but it does – bring up
the old question, *the question meringue.* Never
answered to my satisfaction & hence an opportunity lost
to stumble upon something grand – a sweetheart
with leviathan breasts riding me (appropriately
saddled) we're first across a finish line, a mile ahead
of our rivals, those clumsy fornicators outlandish
with conceit of a metaphysical nature: the piano that plays
our song* coming unstuck in a earthquake, crashing chords
propelling me across the parquet floor of a grand ballroom
into the arms of a woman of indeterminate sex (she's got
the talk but the walk, well, it's not convincing). *My hero,
you've returned. I knew you would.* The return, it would seem,
of a real hero, not just another strutting thespian come
to slit the throat of an evil stepmother with a rubber knife.
*No, darling, this shard of glass in my hand is sharp & it's
for you, payback for that stone.*

*Mack the Knife

Vision

See-saw, Ms Dawe wants to know why
all & nothing are so much past. Wouldn't
have a clue.
           A seer
I'm not nor hogs do I sing
for bristle potential, bacon
left to her:
           pretend mom
with my first wife's passport turning up
at the Brandenburg Gate, an explanation
for total blackout even though relations
are still delicious & in this harness I'm more
than ready for a market run, a lackey's dream
I know,
           but that's the way it is
when Ms Dawe's on a see-saw.

Kellyville

If it's animal you want you've come
to the wrong place. Here:
Bird. Animal's
in Kellyville.

           Where, yesterday,
I was, there to pry
a crack, a ditch
for a cult, a hidy-hole
to probe with finger & tongue
while prettily posing
           so fresh & French
as I won a way to speak a wisdom to a world
where Animal's supreme!
           But here:
Bird. Should have stayed
in Kellyville.

Talent

My talent for strange water doesn't explain why
knives & forks aren't my thing but it does
go some way toward (like a gliding swan as easy as)
an explanation as to why what was seen

as an unsavory act between me &... (Monica,
let's call her that to protect the innocent) by
the incumbent, a Mr. Morris Smith, was
nothing more than the product of an obvious

case of jealously, Smith jilted by M. two days
before the accusation was filed. Butter us
on both sides if, indeed, this is not the case

as unseemly as it might seem. So West
with Smith! And East with gumbo! Who
with us would sup would with hands only!

To Pail

We've come to pail.
Let us rejoice.
And after pail?
An evening of immodesty –
couching Fanny, her seahorse suspension
illuminated like the Eiffel at Christmas.
And then?
Which button do I push for Mohammed?
Selfish bastard, while you've been hammering out
yet another exercise in immodesty
someone's desecrated his tomb. Yes, I know;
& now, since we're in this together,
you're going to tell me which button to push
to bring him to pail.

Haematoma

Rorschach: looks like
pizza; looks like
autopsy now, die later. Cause of death: caught napping
by Florence Cook – chair oracle
smart-ass: Knocked out, Florence,
by your glow. Thar
she blows! My name is Wish
I wasn't in the shit with Florence.

Be War

Be war. Exploit its secret.
Can you be enticed to a hot lickety?
All is not food, only some.
If you have the stuff to topple a lunch, Hail!
If bath you must, be sure to scrub within an inch.
What you get for making deals in dead of night.
Constant clavichord disturbance, a notice should be issued.
Beggar looking in his bowl: still empty.
Hunger experts have become too regional.
International text too integral to itself, i.e.,
      a morsel as bait for Tom & Dick.
Availing ourselves of the delirium of the seventh
   & last appeasement, we acknowledge the suffering
      of the immaculate Joe.

Humiliation

It's just that we the
it's just that we the
pure   of heart   are shamed
by a great pimpled boy soldier
with a gun.

Let's

Let's punish with
glass, wire, tongue, kiss.

Let's bury with
thread, rag, feather, soap.

Let's resurrect with
hammer, pig foot, toothpick, needle.

Don

The slant I'm about to give to the death of Don
is not a slant at all. At all. It's
tall, tall
is the death of Don, a death, Don's,
that resembles ours, yours & mine,
not in the least for ours is short, is squat, is squat
like a hydrant, dogs sniffing, legs lifting, what
we deserve who to Don nothing gave,
who for Don cared not. Great good Don.
Magnificent Don. Small us.

Brother

An acute little sod
comes back for more: Brother,
could you spare a life? I could
but my wife about that
would be oblique, wouldn't settle
for less than an accusation
of pretext. Question: by whom
was she undone & why? By Sam
for a scam: Who stood
for Berlin sat for Dresden, should have been
the other way around, from bacteria
to Andromeda being six lives, not two
as Sam said, a promise as paltry
as pudding on rye, as Himmler
in rafters, Goebbels to blame
for this Ferris wheel toppled on its side, for this Chair-
O-Plane that's thrown its riders to four corners – north,
east, south, west – where angels blow horns to celebrate
the arrival of the dearly departed, fingers in their ears,
this noise the last thing they need. That blasting horn,
I could swear we're about to be overtaken
by a Wehrmacht half-track, storm troopers spitting
dummies as they pass, will soon flush out those gypsies
who live in trees, in the elms on this quiet country road
as from a whole word to a buzz word a crow flies.

Maude

All the reasons for killing Maude
open like doors. Where in Christ's name
do you think you're going? Berlin?
Mombasa? There
to be more than yourself, the whole
of an age? A brilliant idea that, realized,
could change the dead in some
fundamental way. Not sure how. A voice
from beyond, Maude would tell,
one of the reasons for killing her.

Larry

Lingers & won't let go, Larry
is a large sick. Which come-undone
gives entertainment light
& easy. All up for shock,
who are we kidding? Cast blame
like nuggets. And there's the shame
we cut to
the ramp down, no brakes. Scream devils
all ways loose, no lingering. Large sicks
like Larry? Or small? Shock
will sort & tell.

Ralph

A dead dog.
A deep hole.
A piece of rope.
I tied one end around the dog's waist,
the other around mine.
Ralph (I've given him a name)
went in first.
We didn't make it as far as China
but we did come out in a strange city, a city
unlike any I'd ever seen.
Everything – the streets, the buildings, the doors
& windows – was made of polished steel, everything.
And it was bright, much too bright
for my weak eyes.
I soon went blind.
Ralph (who by some miracle has come back to life,
or perhaps he was only sleeping)
was not cut out to be a seeing-eye dog
but he's doing the best he can.

Slander

Ill speak me, you not? Sleaze words
your forte. Overlooked
only if I say so. Body picked up
where left off, thirty-seven years, waiting
to sink into chair. In, yes,
Slade's sights. God knows he'd dearly
love to snap shut more mouths, that gaping one, for
example, of Ms Smith, her reading to scrutiny
never put. And no vessel
to rescue, my wish. Which means not urgent
for brimming glass of Maude's
youth-restoring milk (but that's
another story). Meanwhile
every episode photogenic & please
be done with mixing up, my sex not exchange
for some color – Orange? Vermillion? – but kept
as sparkle at least, a reminder
of those heady brothel days, submission
to an iron maid unthinkable, never
on cards. And in that tiny closet
where the queen mother lived, her audience
a prelude to intimacy – one dress, threadbare,
& a dozen down-at-heel shoes (tried
to give them away to those faded taxi dancers
at Table Nine – slap, slap, slap). Not quite
a zeppelin experience, but almost: who would,
like you, ill speak me but in one ear
& out the other, sleaze words gone.

Bridge

If it wasn't on a horse it was on a camel that I crossed
the Pont Neuf, figuring a penny farthing fate
or fete or faith. Faith? No, cross it out
& settle on... fete. Fete
of Action Beauties Without Peer. So proclaimed
in '68 by D. Donald, eminent critic, friend & mentor
who the advice below gave & it for years proved sound
though unsound now: Give yourself
to the men of Mersa Fatma who'll have you
for a hostage that no wife will have the wherewithal
to buy you out of. And thus be spared
that perennial question: *Why must sex with you*
always be an instant classic? The first
to come to mind – because the covered wagon days
are long over – completely unacceptable; & the second –
because I chickened out on that jump from the 10th floor
window of the J.L. Hudson Department Store in
downtown Detroit on January 10, 1937 – stupidly
provocative. Of course the pleasure of the ox at pulling
was rendered null & void & in its place: the flaring nostrils
of an outraged bull which, hopefully, I'll have the courage
to face naked, no Suit of Light for wives to fight over,
to tear that brilliance into shreds, Action Beauties at it
tooth & claw. It was on a mule that I crossed.

Knocking

Fatima's hand knocking on a door
that opens to a wolf. At your service, sir, my home
your own. And now no doubt you'll tell me why
Holland sank & likewise Tel Aviv & why
oppression always originates with those who extract privilege
from fools like me, my hard slog at cremation stalls
deemed not hard enough even though I worked them, the
dead, for all they were worth, inflation
my undoing apparently. Bought
when I should have sold, my fate
to languish in my glaring miscalculations
as to cause & effect, which
begat which, etc. "Sad picture,
are you my life?" – a dunce
in a house of straw.

SWF

What I have to offer – a circus, a war, a fall
from a tower – apparently not enough. What's needed,
they insist, is a power to besmirch, to shelter askew
& a year at lard.

                So out of this life
will I soon be leaving at a trot? Or
walking? In any case certainly not deserving
of a look-in, an unread petitioner perpetually
at the ready.

             "Pop out!"
I'll shout, as did the derelict ejected
from the Corston Bridal Boutique. "Stuff you
with your veils & bodice effrontery, I didn't want
to marry anyway!"

                Lily, who loves me for the way
I squat? She'll have to wait
for the next round when what is obviously the case
will be emphatically stated over a megaphone: *Sexual*
(read artistic)repression is a weapon of authoritarian,
patriarchal culture.

                Ok, that should nail it but of course
it won't. Their failure *to support a husbandry*
that imbues its every act with nutrients
of a spiritual nature is endemic.

                Unjustified,
this complaint? It's just that, mouth cropped
past all sense, I'd at least like a drum roll as I'm sent,
crawling, to bed without my supper.

Harp

Am I that harp?
Am I that harp hung by its strings
in that old oak tree on the corner
of Hastings & Vine? – gallants pimping
mellifluous sisters, a fee
for a feel, traffic
at a standstill.
               Molly
my stripper, scissors east & scissors west
to cut my clothes.
               Good
if we let the dog run cold. Better
if you Yes me at my well, Yes
to my face in a bucket. Best
if you acknowledge that I'm covered for chicken
& covered for lamb & for every meat
that you might care to name
                        on the corner
of Hastings & Vine where I'm plucked
for a fee in that old oak tree.

Whispering

The whisper of ontology –
more like a hiss & nothing to do with
      the ancient art of horse whispering.
In my opinion there's nothing more odious than an ontology
      of horse whispering.

Whispering to a horse on a roundup
      is a useless exercise.
Likewise to a bucking bronco at a rodeo.

When I went to the congress of Horse Whisperers
  to give my paper on the ontology of Cow Whispering
      I had to shout to be heard.

Leopard

Eyes the yellow of crime scene tape
if this leopard is innocent
my name is Barry the Bald

though I still have hair in patches
& ample hat & coat with collar too. The
largest example of now? The smallest
of then? Ocean
comes over the hill. The tumbled walls
of Jericho. Ship oars & forthwith
up from the deep
in a diving bell: a book, read it
cover to cover. *On the Criminality of Leopards* by
Bald, Barry.

Gourmet

Open that box
& take out that heart, slice & serve
to this tart in a stitch
at your nerve, this Nelly as naked
as slag. O singular
& most grievous pomp could here
any fiddle stick? Could mud in any eye
achieve some divinity however fleeting? And if
the answer is Yes should we then kneel
in divinity also, hearts on our sleeves, some sacrament
to commence?

Miracle

I am Miracle burn
    by Miracle 25 yrs.
I was born thing.
Have been hard for me.
Any money is not too small.
I don't want to go into rubbery
    that is why I am begging.
Bible say give
    and it shall be giving Unto you.
This is my number: +324607663438

A Monk

Let's carry the monk a bit further, see if he remembers
who he is, what he's supposed to represent.

What does a dropped monk look like? A snuffed candle?
A stick in mud? A dropped monk?

A penny for an unwanted thought is the precise value of
a monk. In this example the thought (or in this case the
question) is: If a monk is dropped how far will he fall?

Redemption

Booths on every corner, ten dollars for ten minutes.
Liberian Dollars. A money exchange booth? Over there,
but you'll need photo ID. A photo booth? Over there, but
it only takes Ethiopian Birr.

No Djinns

When I scuttled off to the kitchen to find something
to gnaw on a cook for the wealthy said: To Hunger
comes trumpery if you continually surround it
with liturgical chatter. So, no sacrament for me (I don't
deserve one) & as for SEX: wolf it down quick
before the others arrive with their lamps
& the perennially stupid question: No djinns,
should we keep rubbing? Please, don't pester me
with your Greed. I'm already
up to my neck in Shame, & Seduction, who wants
to marry me off to a tailor's son, is still refusing
to give Want its due – some rags
to swaddle in. Slave to master: this punishment
I don't deserve: Collared & marched to the cherry end
of a cul-de-sac where Honour lies in wait
for its next victim. Cause of death: Master's switch
from switch to cane.

Seer

Where you get them visions from?
I'd rather focus on the destruction of genius. Ok,
that's enough. And now
a round of applause

from the windows of Holland
for the ceiling of France,
from the doors of Greece
for the floor of Spain. Ok,

that's enough. It's already fallen,
the sky, & what's left of it, this bit of metal,
I'll put in my pocket, a coin for later,
for a slice of salami. That's

what you want, isn't it – your salami
sliced? Because the knife in your belt
is hopelessly dull; it might
cut butter but... meat? –

pig foot, baby, & punch head pie,
church loot, baby, & a bare-faced lie,
jackboot, baby, & a squashed horsefly;
if it's my time to die stuff me quick

with sugar & spice,
with milk & honey,
with words not cheap, them words
I say my visions with.

Sissy C Sissy Do

For muscular men it's a must to give
a max answer. So obvious
that you've been carelessly worn, an irresistible attraction
to back-of-the-bus thugs, their dribs & drabs of slaps
pinpointing the greenest part of an otherwise
sprawling vision.
    Too bad
(no sleeping dogs for you) you just didn't leave it
for them to wrestle out among themselves, a halt thereby
to every race. O what you wouldn't give
to do some spooning with this lot, such froth
they whip as scissors & paper
settle into seem.
    Short
of a last stand, what are you saving up for? More
gruel? Enough gel for a six day week? Is it time to lamb
but you can't, that boss you knelt to coming back
to haunt you?
     Might as well insert your key in (into?)
Miss Fancy Fine's sky-blue door, love like a tight cannon
the moment you show. It's a five star tease. It's much
too confidential to spell it out here. As much
as you'd like to no answer by sissies need be given.

Explications

Willy to Ron explains that when
we beat our drums for mice we're sure
that our nights of sick are Schultz, he
of the nails that scratch our blacks & whites
as we're bashed into brackets. Which hearing,
Jasmine to Sally whispers far better would be
to thump our doctors silly in their presumptuous
wigwams, an end thus put to shoes
in school! To sled burials! To every
shimmering man thing! A sentiment
that Sue shares, confiding to Fatima that far
too many are we in this balloon's basket to rise
to God, best out with those who refuse to learn
the lessons of minarets. Gregorius concurs
but with the addendum that the Humbles
with their angelic tum-tum be rid as well, eliminated
with hook & ladder as they the fat chew. Not
so, shouts Nell, underdog champion, your style
of dribs & drabs with bibs on is no jewel
in a bijoux box, is but, thinly disguised, the argument
of golden calf as made to a john who a pimp follows
to a sister with sea horse nipples. And may he win
near & far with full meaning, sly with indifference
of no account exclaims Bob the Tall to Sue
of the Apple Bob, her Radio Amerika fallback forever
failing at conjunctions, this a typical example as Ron to
Willy it's but another Big Never, page red & page blank
being as always & in the face of drums for mice equal.

On Bells

On bells: ring speech: *Give you one*
up side the head. Always happens
when you do a box character. Who took (he did)
the grave patch? Trench hero: when he sees blue grass

he sees black. Cancer twins: we're on our way
to Mum's. Homeward bound: two gals
in saddle shoes. What's this? It's the lather
of memorabilia. We'd better skirt

the speech-clad neighbours, that throat
too white not to slit. If it's a good death
we'd better lock it in. Big Time
somewhere else. Embark on the *Rex*

while we still have a chance. Pipe
them aboard: Miss Peek-a-boo & her retinue
of Goth girls. Fashion statement: gambit
of a tomb sweeper, catwalk gambol

on a high sea, a North Atlantic mid-winter
rage, some fool sailor offering sex
to she-male mermaids. Could end up
a quarter deck frolic with hybrids

hot to score. No more, I say, no more
needling (nudging) because already they got
so they don't move no more. So why you went & done
that bob's-your-uncle business? Easy: French cuffs

invite a lay. O classic dad your length of teeth
please explain – kettle my marriage, too much tea
in the night-safe sector, a candy ass servitude
I couldn't tolerate. O how it hurt

that bite, plunder for that something boss
who turned out fraudulent, etymology
his hustle. Earwigs mine, what I listen
I speak as centerfold, snug

in a trench, Great War aria, allegiance
to none, no grave patch for this boy. When
I see blue grass I see Kentucky, Big Time
for ring boys, *up side they head.*

Hole

As soon as I've dug a hole
no matter where or how deep
there's always some asylum type in my face
demanding bipolarity.
                    The hole in one
is one, is a singularity, you fool, so please remove
your dubious self from my honourable presence
now!
        Else
hoopla, naughty girl
to cut your hair, spanked maid
your gig. And that's not all; there's

chicken counting in Dubai, wholesale
rummage, everyone
selling cheap. So thus informed
be doubly quick away

like a rootless babe, danger men, my men
on your case; not for you a pretty turn around
if you persist. Not my problem
that you learned to talk

when talk was cheap, though to be fair
I should have walking, should have come
to court stained, pabulum
to a fool fed.

Fathers & Sons

"I'm catalogue & canticle." Nonsense, you're simply
at it again: indulging in yet another of those all-
or-nothing post mortems, the purpose of which
is a text grab. And, yes, I do know
that you're naked under that sheet. Hiding, dare
I assume, from the ghost of Lotte Lenya who might,
provoked, give you a thumbs down: back to Berlin
in your birthday suit, going speed
that cuts nothing, at least not close enough
to initiate a triumph over that argument
you lost to me: that my perishing queen did,
in fact, have nothing to do with your litigious
life style, if that's what you could call it, that
would-be eternal ride in a see-through glass carriage
that shattered when I laughed at the mess you made
of the black swan on the *operating* table, your *surgical*
gown splattered with blood, a kitchen knife
in your shaking hand, the whole thing
but a failed attempt to impress me, to convince me
that you're catalogue & canticle.

Shuffle

Shuffle me ever so slowly forward, one
cm, two cm. ECT at six
point nine M: dapper Cuban doctor – black hair, black
suit, black shirt, black tie, black shoes – at the control
panel, ME-108.
                Lightning
in threes, Storm Trooper collar.
                      No-name morning, memory
out with the bathwater.
                Ba ba black sheep
I have no wool, mummy
in cold must lie, on ice kept
for a better (more memorable) day as into the fray
I'm shuffled, one cm, two cm.

Ask

Ask: what voice (this voice?) will stand scrutiny
by the whores of literature? Don't know. So what
should we do? More verbals? No, we've
verballed enough. We must refuse to follow that oaf
with the right leg & the wrong ear. No
choice! Forward
march! Fair trade? – a scratch
for an itch? You bitch, tell me on what frequency
do you hear when telltale hits
aren't the slaps we believe were left
to devices remote, not yours?
                              Say (we will)
what you want to hear, that what we hear
are the songs that the tomb players proposed
& we *did* accept with the proviso that
no word would be left to hang unsaid like
a plea for leniency for a debauched elder
with drool on his bib: Golly,
was that a wog in your bed?
What manner of sex?
Did toes twinkle?
                        So long ago, means
nothing now. So off you go,
wrong leg, right ear.

Fleshpots

Let's gull a sham, a cook
with crow! Such motor skills
in this we could reckon
in the honey class, be prized

above all! – mutton
at the cocktail hour not
out of context. No, nor likewise
those claims made for clams

so voraciously consumed
by gourmets on the gamin
circuit, Place Pigalle, etc.
where the venery of Iscariot

who rejoices in petticoat
is celebrated with a tethering
of goats, their grazing
immortalized in fiction, under wraps

for later when the motion
is called for: gutter candles
before the money changers
take tumbles like lovers

swept off their feet
by skin brag, skin brag
in a nest of nails where Insomnia
grown insolent insists

on geyser, on a constantly
shuffling military, on a traffic in lace
on corsets so tight
they gull a sham.

Compassion

for the Fur Lackeys —so busy clamouring for a chance
   to paint more spots on Stephanie Guelph's Guernsey
   cow that they've forgotten to decorate
   the other animals & will be punished
   accordingly;
for the Amen Hookers – ten thousand blue men
   in a little black book, & what do they do?
   They rescue Gaga from the Gooks;
for the Ha'penny Slammers – wrestled to the ground
   by a sperm papa, all they can think of
   is to hire more shoppers;
for the Snigger Babas – making do with less
   than perfect spunk while they hiss the names
   of those spent villages – Jath, Nalgonda, Kalyani –
   to which they'll never return;
for the Little Morbids – as serene as children
   in coffins, who'd guess that their yields
   have a yawl factor: Howdy! Apple! Bang!
for the Pulpit Hopefuls – wheel-chaired into
   a snake pit, have they failed to grasp
   that all containers (themselves included)
   are ritual containers?
for the Chacmool Sluts – withered old men perched,
   pieta-like, on their mistresses' laps, couldn't
   care (or so they say) how butter-soft
   their mouth-watering poo poos are;
for the Bala Boys – sprawled in puddles,
   have a leakage problem that won't be solved
   before the show's over & by then
   it will be too late.

Saturday, December 7, 2010

My task for today: describe how urine looks & smells
    when it *issues* from a ghost, a cow, a man.

And then to make a record, a *clinical* record & put
    my name to it.

Like watching a plumber expose pipe: X18+ contains
    sexually explicit material.

I doubt it. I doubt that your Jesus could become even
    more obscene than He already is.

This image, quick, cover it with hair, with thick red hair
    before someone sees it

For you: snippets of carpet, Persian, possibly a flyer & if so
    where to?

That the sheet we've folded is twisted like a rope says
    something: long enough to hang.

Remembering that we still have nothing on which
    to hang our trophies I've strung a clothesline from one end
    of the dining room to the other.

But what I'd dearly love to do: fill the bedroom
    with the hull, ribs exposed, of a wrecked ship.

Turn a corner & there you are, again, no more prepared
    for a *parsimonious sonority* than you were before.

What you've just done on the piano can only be described
    as *interjacent.*

To your injury – *fecundated* – here's an added insult: seed
   as in *gone to*.

Nothing wrong with the denominations – 10, 20, 50, 100 –
   it's to the things to which they're attached that I object.

In one pan, a *phyllopod*, & in the other, to balance it,
   a *phylum*.

Thus, for posterity: the history of today.

Hometown

Population 1950: 1,849,568; 2010: 916,952

2010: 33,000 vacant houses.

Crack-heads (paid?) to torch abandoned houses.

The Hantz Group, a financial holding company, plans
  to buy thousands of the Motor City's cheap acres & turn
  them into what may be the world's biggest urban farm.

2010: average price of a home in Detroit – $5700.

Some say it's a sign of weakness.

On the morning of December 11, 2002, more than 100
  residents of a city-owned apartment building in down-
  town Detroit were subjected to a mass eviction into
  freezing temperatures & icing drizzle.

How sweet it is to be loved by you.

August 5, 2009: a 78 year old man resisting eviction from
  his apartment at a senior citizen complex was shot
  multiple times by Detroit police.

Tell me what I did wrong.

November 21, 2009: unburied bodies piling up in the city
  mortuary (it reached 70 this year) is the latest & perhaps
  most appalling indignity heaped on the people of Detroit.

65-70% of homicides are drug related.

Deliver the letter the sooner the better.

Its violent crime rate of 1,220 violent crimes committed
  per 100,000 people earns it top spot on Forbes.com's
  list of most dangerous cities.

Among the 25 largest U.S. cities Detroit is the 6th highest
  for violent crimes.

Homicides were the 4th leading cause of death in Detroit
  last year – after heart attacks, cancer & strokes.

2006: murders 418; rapes 593; robberies 7240; aggravated
  assaults 13143; burglaries 18134; larceny/theft 21287;
  car theft 22917.

2010: car thefts up 83%; robberies up 50%; burglaries up
20%; property destruction up 42%.

Buy yourself a shotgun.

Street gangs: Bloods; Crips; Latin Counts; Sureno 13; Cash
Flow Posse; Zone 8; Count Repo; Cobras; Vice Lords;
18th Street; Dexter Boys; Folks; 7 Mile; Latin Disciples;
Maniac; Chaldean Mafia; Latin Kings; Spanish Cobras...

Bike gangs: Highwaymen; Hell's Angels; Bandidos...

They'll tell you a story of sadness.

Unemployment: 50%. Officially, Detroit's unemployment
rate is just under 30%. But the mayor & local leaders
are suggesting a far more disturbing figure – the actual
jobless rate, they say, is just under 50%.

Your love don't pay my bills.

December 17, 2009. Nearly one in two workers in Detroit
are unemployed, according to a report by the Detroit News.

I can tell by the way you hang your head.

Per capita income in Detroit in the last full census was
$14,717, in the U.S: 21,587.

WE ACCEPT FOOD STAMPS

Since 1990 the auto industry donated $77 million to
federal candidates & political parties.

I heard it through the grapevine.

2002: Before becoming White House Chief of Staff,
Andy Card was a GM executive.

GM: billions are being spent on SUV advertising. A
misguided tax loophole rewards buyers of extra
large SUVs.

Better shop around.

4000 closed factories:

Ford Motor Co. Headquarters – abandoned;

Ford Piquette Plant – abandoned;

Mack Avenue Chrysler Plant – abandoned;

Fisher Body Plant 21 – abandoned

Studebaker Piquette Ave. Plant – burned to ground;

Dodge Main – demolished...

Getting ready for the heartache to come.

October 24, 1988: With the press of a button at 5:47pm
Detroit Mayor Dennis Archer dropped the J.L. Hudson
Department Store from his city's skyline (tallest
department store in the country & second in floor
space to Macy's in NY).

I feel all choked up inside.

Mayor Kwame Kilpatrick jailed, charged with nearly
a dozen felonies.

That's what I want – money!

Councilwoman Monica Conyers admitted taking bribes
from a developer to change her vote on a major city
contract.

I can really shake 'em down.

Five officials charged with multiple felonies for
embezzling public education funds.

May 21, 2009: Emergency Financial Manager Robert
Bobb is planning to close 29 more schools this year
& another 20 next year.

Standing in the shadows of love.

Of those children tested (2097) 6.2% had elevated lead
levels. If all children of this age had been tested then
48556 would have elevated levels.

I've got sunshine on a cloudy day.

In Detroit during 2003 151 patients under the 18 years
of age per 10,000 population were admitted for a
preventable hospitalization diagnosis.

Leave your picture behind; I've kissed it a thousand times.

17.4% of births in Detroit were to teens. 13.4% of live
births in Detroit are low birth weight births. The
disparity between the black infant mortality rate &
the rate for white infants has grown wider in the last
five years (in Michigan – 5.2 for white, 17.3 black).

Why you do me like you do?

                                    Paris/Woodford 2009/2010

SELECTED POEMS

Tall Tales

Get a raconteur ready.
If Niger stood up & were told how tall would it be?
And, having heard, would we by then have heard enough
    to hear how tall that Niger is?
Or has Niger stood up already told too often limp by
Lilliputian tellers in prose that's flat & mud-brown?
Of which, such a teller, there is one in London, a lazy lout.
And one in Berlin, a beggar with a single sleazy fact.
And three in Bern, belittlers. Overlook these

& get a real raconteur ready with enough material to start
in rooster-red a Niger cult that crows upon a post that's
tall enough to let us hear from it
the little way that we, thus crowed, have yet to hear
assuming
of course that we at rending veils (& mixing metaphors)
are as pig-snout perfect as we are led to think we are; &
then:

that final push that puts the Lilliputians (the boys
from the men) in their place – our Niger stood up
as tall in the telling as it's told!

TKO

Round one: the boxer dances out from his corner, in one of his cumbersome gloves a tiny golden key with which he must open a small golden box that sits on a stool in the ring's center &, the box open, must remove from its red velvet interior a pale blue robin's egg & carry it to his still-seated opponent in the opposite corner.

Round two: the opponent must return the egg to the box, close & lock it & carry the key to the first boxer who, meanwhile, has returned to his corner.

Round three: the first boxer dances out…

Square One

Not there yet. Why try? Instead, a vow
of stasis: render progress null
& void, render back to the fathers,
mothers before. And then relax. On
for size & it seems to fit – an easy world
of sit & watch, of done with dance
around a maypole that extends
into what? – a sky chock-a-block
with UFOs, & through them, steering
a hazardous course: The Perennial
(read Parental) Airship that we, long
tow lines, sheer plunge into Yangtze
turbulence, must, are still, have
never stopped pulling. "Pull
harder!" – a voice from where? – from
on high where of late so many
have gathered. "Prairie
buns!" – Any relation to the "Pull
harder" of a moment ago? Probably not. Probably
a new task: pull schooners
into a tight circle, scalping
Redskins, the whole bloody (rivers
of it) shebang – Death Valley, Donner
Pass, "Prairie Buns!"

A Shop

Blindfolds on pegs. The clients make their selections,
try them on in dressing rooms, take them to a counter to
have them wrapped, extract coins from pockets or
purses &, on the way out, drop them into the
proprietor's tin cup.

The Beautiful Blond

lying on her stomach gazing at the sea is not aware of
the old sailing ship that rises from the sand immediately
behind her &, sea-bound, somehow contrives to secure
her for its figurehead.

Public Execution

A full moon, & under it – hundreds of black figures on
ice skates zigzagging down the frozen lanes of Venice
to a rendezvous in the Grand Canal. It's here, in a small
circle of unfrozen water, that the swan glides
majestically; & around it, on their knees on ice – a dozen
monks with candles working feverishly to stay
the tightening noose.

Pragmatism

Epaulets or sexy underwear, it's all the same to George
of the Tower although, having second thoughts, he
decides that epaulets in a sudden thundershower might
afford him more protection than madam's drawers.

Empire Rumours

My aunt
was a Miss Jane twice & my uncle
was thoroughly contentious with rumors that kept
me scratching, a partisan of the perfect
bust & would, he insisted, upon
closer inspection, eventually vent
this unwholesome lust upon the person of his poor
Miss Jane twice who would then, her
worst fear realized, have ample cause to call
this welcome/unwelcome intrusion her *other*
ocean come to this far-from-perfect-shore when in fact
it was nothing but a series of glass coffins capable
perhaps of flight but each smaller
than its predecessor until at the end
she who was a Miss Jane twice could hold the last
ten thousand in the palm of her once-perfect hand.

The Float

Tomorrow is Homecoming Day, so we decide to make a
float for the big parade. We borrow a wagon from my
landlady's son. Search-out & bring-back missions are
deployed. Inspiration is found in bins & in a pile of
discarded timber. Soon the wagon is bristling with
sticks, an eight foot high porcupine on wheels; & on its
quills we impale rotten oranges, apples, grapefruit,
cucumbers, heads of lettuce and long slabs of rancid
bacon. A rope is attached to the handle so that all four
of us – one African American, one Chicano, one long-haired
beatnik & one wise guy New York punk (this is
heavy redneck country, Athens, Ohio, 1959) – can pull it. The
next afternoon, via side streets, we manage to manoeuver
our contribution to school spirit in between
one of the floats (two crepe-paper footballers) & the
sorority queen who follows it in a white Cadillac
convertible. We become her float! And pull it (the
others are all motorized) the entire length of the parade
route. The fraternity boys, watching from the footpaths,
are dying to kick ass; they can hardly restrain
themselves, & my art teacher (watching from a
window) gives me an A for the semester.

The Thief

Paul, Rob & I have asked the forest rangers for
permission to climb Mt. Nyiragongo, Africa's only
active volcano. Yes, but it's too late now; we'll have to
wait until tomorrow. We can camp in the reception
building. So we roll out our sleeping bags side by side
in the center of the room & carefully tuck our valuables
under them. This is the Zaire; one can't be too careful.
The night is pitch black, not even a hint of a moon.
We're exhausted and soon fall asleep. Suddenly I'm
awakened by someone shouting: "Voleur! Voleur!" (Thief!
Thief!). I sense something, a human form, hovering over
me. I go for the throat. I've got the
bastard in a strangle hold! His hands & others are
pummelling me. I'm being beat ferociously. There's a
great rolling & thrashing about. As I tighten my hold I
begin to sense that something is wrong. This thief has
a huge bushy beard. Most of the African men in Zaire, if
they do have beards, keep them neatly trimmed.
"Paul?" I ask. "Phil?" he gasps "Paul? Phil?" queries
Rob. Paul has had a nightmare about thieves.

Totem

A tenth-floor suicide lands on the shoulders of a ninth-floor suicide & the ninth on an eighth & so on to the very bottom of the building (there is even a first-floor suicide who lands on the shoulders of a man standing on the footpath); & so we have with these frustrated suicides a swaying tower of acrobats, a living totem of surprised faces; & when the man on the footpath (who has been waiting for a light to change & who is very strong) begins to cross the street there is a great tooting of horns & a huge round of applause.

Possessions

A man who carries all of his possessions in his mouth
sits down on a park bench (he's naked), uses both
hands to pry his jaws open, reaches in, extracts a pair of
shoes & some clothes, gets dressed & then, protected
against the evening chill, reaches in again & pulls out
his supper, a hamburger, & gobbles it down.

Runners

A runner wearing fish shoes gets across a river well
ahead of his competitors who are wearing rabbit shoes.
But will he win the race? As the course consists of
three river crossings & three bodies of dry land it's
anyone's guess.

Wheels

A man on wheels rolls out into the world & proceeds to execute a series of dazzling manoeuvers – spins, leaps, skids, cartwheels, on-a-dime stops & turns… But the people in the world, some of them bowled over, are not amused. A crisis team is called in, & the team leader, a most eloquent fellow, persuades a man to return to the psychiatric hospital from which he has recently escaped. Within an hour a man is back on his ward.

But what to do with such a man? Injected with the most powerful drugs he's still out of control – spins, leaps, cartwheels… And so, after a thorough evaluation, it's decided that the only cure for a man is to schedule him for a *wheelotomy*, i.e., to surgically remove the offending wheels.

It only takes a few minutes, & the world is surely much better for it – a no longer menacing man who stands on his own two feet.

A Drive with Dr. Plotz

The eminent psychiatrist, Dr. Eva Plotz, has taken her
patient, young Anthony Glitz, for a drive in her
Plotzmobile. As you know, a Plotzmobile is a
recreational vehicle made to order for the psychiatric
profession. A rugged, multipurpose machine, today we see it
performing one of its main functions – to return a lunatic's
demons to the woods from which they came.
Young Anthony seems elated by the prospect of getting
rid of his & has filled the vehicle with a warm glow of
gratitude.

And now they arrive at the heart of the forest, a
valentine-shaped patch of scorched grass
surrounded by venerable sky-touching trees,
their gnarled branches
prolific with hissing serpents. It's here that young
Anthony's demons will be given lollipops & left, poor
things, to fend for themselves. So long out of the
woods, how will they survive? Like wild animals born
in captivity, they'll no doubt be devoured by their wild
brethren as soon as the Plotzmobile has driven off.
Such a prospect is too horrible to contemplate, & young
Anthony will have none of it! He stamps his feet &
insists that all of his demons be taken back to the city.
Dr. Plotz, unprepared for this eventuality, threatens &
reasons & begs, but to no avail. Young Anthony prevails.

And here they are returning to civilization – young
Anthony, Dr. Plotz & a host of demons. Difficult to
count how many, but there must be at least a thousand.
Have they multiplied, or have some of the wild brethren

clambered, uninvited, into the Plotzmobile? And poor Dr. Plotz, what a difficult time she's having, especially at the traffic lights where she must shift the gears & work the clutch with a great hairy Glug sitting in her lap & a Snotgut, slippery with slime, curled up at her feet &, look, there's a Nicknoodle making a magpie's nest of her expensive coiffure. Hopelessly snarled with the paraphernalia of madness – bits of glass & bottle caps & silver spoons – what will her colleagues say when they see it?

Boxing

At two o-clock the widows get up from their naps & go for a round. A round of what? Boxing. That they may have a few mementoes from this life in the next, each day at this time they put a frayed ribbon or a faded photograph or a well-thumbed love letter into a box & send it to God.

Tough Luck

Because it's had its glasses broken in a bar-room brawl a piano can't find its stool – so must play standing up. Standing music from a blind piano – too much for the patrons, & before long one of them, a punch-drunk ex-boxer, puts his fist in motion & breaks the piano's nose.

Tables

If you break down his rabbit he'll show you his hat.
This hat is an utmost, a furtherance, a figment. And
everyone, bar none, is wearing it, this figment,
furtherance, utmost of a hat. And under it, everyone
thus covered, we're all participating in the same
activity; here, around this table, we're all sharing some
mutton, carving it up, for one as for many, into
portions, bite-sized, for consumption. Around others,
other tables, it might be chicken, in pieces, for each the
same, not one at variance; or it might be a rabbit that's
being divvied up & placed with democratic fervor into
mouths situated around some other table. And there, at
that table, the rabbit table, if you break it down they'll
show you a hat, the one that we're all wearing.

Of Tubs, Sailors & Inflation

Tub prices up. Rub
down. Which combination, up & down, makes it easy
for a body, any body, to get a proper break – as easy
as pie & without the help of some lethal slap-
stick heart making pulp of its host, the corpse
of the text. But don't think
for even a minute that you'll get off with just
a light sentence – "See
Dick run." – it's
serious, this breaking business, it's
much more than just a matter of picking up
the nearest chunk of throbbing muscle & using it
to clear a mob of rowdy sailors from a house
of ill repute before you can say "See
Dick perform an act of cunnilingus
on Jane" because that's
where she wants it, your tongue; she's had
her bath & her massage & now… but it's
serious, this breaking business; proper breaks
don't grow on trees, they don't come cheap. Unlike
those sailors from the boat in your tub they can't
be had for just a song such as this one that manages,
but just barely, to get back, the proverbial
tail-swallowing serpent, to its opening
statement – the rising price of tubs.

What I Do in a Horn

In a horn I hear
what I'm told to say, which, after I've said it,
isn't very much.

In a horn as much
as the air can bear it
I commend myself.

In a horn I have
only one option: to huff
& puff.

In a horn I concede
to the Mi & to the Fa
but not to the So.

In a horn I put them
to a rigorous test, my lip-smacking revelations, a few
pass.

In a horn I find
the false notes & put them
out of their misery.

In a horn I reach
for a brook, to strangle it before it babbles
my shame, dirty & rotten.

In the horn I examine the stomach contents
of a fruit-fly & come to this conclusion: food
is a fool's game.

In a horn there's a knot
that you can't untie; I can,
but I won't.

In a horn there is
no fear; I've consigned it
to the string section.

In a horn I've drawn
a line; cross
at your own risk.

In a horn I open
a bag; it's full of dirt, enough
to fill the crack.

In a horn I'm naked, black
stars on white skin, ready
for anything.

In a horn I sleep
in my clothes, leafy garments
protected by thorns.

In a horn, despite
appearances, I'm never
flaccid.

In a horn I gather
the evidence against myself; it's
water-tight.

In a horn I swim
with angels; they get their wings wet
but that doesn't stop them.

In a horn I keep
my finger on the pulse; it never rains
on my parade.

In a horn I practice
the discipline of the tortoise, the rapture
of the hare.

In a horn I manipulate
the seasons & even the hour; it's always
summer, high noon, a clear sky.

In a horn I see to it
that all the lights
are always on.

In a horn I remove the principle
component from the machine that makes death
such a viable proposition.

In a horn I fully condone
what I've done, am doing, have yet
to do.

In a horn I'm more
often than not.

In a horn I get
my just desserts: plenty.

In a horn I'm home
safe.

Mad About Me

The total indifference of, say,
a Toby Knowles, no
relation, is what they pretend out
on their stoops & balconies after, severely
provoked, I've challenged them to a hunt – "Pick up
a feed & give it a credible swallow!" – this in response
to their insufferable calling out to one another whenever
I pass on sea-legs swaying home from a war with dire
leviathans –"Now there's
a health!" – meaning me of course (I swear
I'll live to see these lubbers navigable) on my way
to clear up some verbal confusions between, say,
daughter & slaughter, easy enough to make
such a simple mistake given the din
of the neighbourhood, everyone, as I've said, out
on stoops & balconies mad
about me that I'm not dead yet that I haven't
gone down to the sea in a ship yet, having heard
from some fool on Radio Judas that
I was finally in the locker, that my deep death
was the kind they could study at their leisure, for
example, while swallowing their words while pretending
the total indifference of, say,
a Roby Bowles, no relation.

The Ritual of the Stick

Tell us, Mother, for how much longer must we continue to

Hold ourselves up, standing?

Break & run– impossible.

An encroachment: to trespass upon the property
        or rights of another.

Once set in motion, the machine...

As above, so below – this drumming.

These people got rhythm, blind men tapping, tick
        tack toe, etc.

Of sticks, their satiety.

Plenty more where this came from.

An abundance, to say the least.

How much more than our money's worth?

As a matter of procedure – hot licks.

Mother, tell us, is our meat sweet?

Stripped down, Father, to a bare essential.

Your pound, gentlemen, of flesh.

But, gentlemen, our generosity *does* have a limit.

Too long, Father, in Your Church of the Interminable
    Flagellation.

Is there in this, somewhere, a hallelujah?

Obviously, a passage to something, but to what?

Whether, Mother, to come or go? In one direction
    only; there's no turning back.

A stick to end (at the end of) all sticks.

The next leg of this journey, as straight as a...

Not monkey business this, stick business.

A mind of its own, this stick.

Try it on for size, this stick.

Beyond explanation, how far can one go with one, a
    stick?

That silly smile wiped off, Mother with a stick.

Scissors cut paper, sticks... flesh.

It's just a game – pick-up sticks, & hit.

The last thing that we want to hear, Father, is a stick.

In the final analysis, it's nothing but a stick.

Gathering one the hard way, an authenticity.

A bit of turbulence here, a kind of weather.

Tucked in, with a vengeance.

It's true, we're in a stew.

It tends, alas, to set askew.

One can get used to anything so they say, but to this?

Could it become a habit, impossible to break?

Work getting done. Is it God's? What's the rush?

Many called, few (for this) chosen.

A truth, o blood of the lamb, in this cliché.

Taking precedence over what? – as a matter of fact, over
      our lives.

Free, a death thrown in.

Out of touch, o would that we were.

But you've yet to get it right, gentlemen; we're
      still alive.

The body count? – count ours?

Down for the count – 2210.

O Champion of the Redundant Blow, tell us…

O tell us, Father, when, by Your watch, will this
      be finished?

Quadruply, multi-dimensionally broken.

On January 2, 1991, in Radigon, Bihar State, India, Philip Hammial & his
wife were savagely beaten by seventeen members of the CPM.

A Funeral

Like an ancient warrior carried to a pyre on his shield
our poet laureate is carried to his on a book, his
Selected Poems. A tiny man on a thin volume, it won't
take long for the fire to do its work.

A Basket Case

What's this coming over the hill? Six shaggy goats, two
by two, harnessed to a tiny wagon. And what's in the
wagon? Tied in a sitting position, legs crossed, slumped
over, huge-bellied, a mountain of a man, the God of the
Goats being taken where? To the hospital in the valley.
Why? Because he's broken. What happened? He fell
from the sky. Can he be mended? Probably not, but
don't tell the goats.

Grand Prix

Out in front by several lengths – a monastery of monks on
a bicycle built for twenty-two. But steadily gaining, pumping
furiously, not to be beaten, here they come – a nunnery of
nuns on a bicycle built for seventy-six. And now they're
wheel & wheel, & now the nuns are
pulling ahead. The nuns are going to win!

On the East Hills Line

Approaching Turrella, we come upon a row of fence-
sitters – about 300 men in blue business suits astraddle a
high wire fence that goes for miles. They've been
here for years, we're told, & are fed (can you see the
tubes?) intravenously. Shit & piss dribbling down the
wire, once a week a crew comes to hose it down.

from Fin de Siecle

Rise & Shine

Holding a bouquet of deep-blue violets, he rose to the
position of a middle-ranking communications
functionary. No mean achievement for a man whose
parents were poor farmers, & now from a comfortable
seat on the top deck of a horse-drawn omnibus
approaching the corner of the Boulevard d'Enfer & the
rue Campagne-Premiere he reminds his readers that
suspicion, doubt & feebleness of spirit spell death to
love, but they find this well-meant observation extremely
offensive & slam the book shut (crushing the
violets) before he can offer an apology.

Fishing with Worms

Uncovering a meaningless statement that points to the
site of a libidinal drive, he went at once to the Carreau du
Temple & selected the *sociolect* that would justify
his frequent trips to the Hotel des Etrangers where, some
months later, he would be forced to admit to an addiction
to those high dramas that invariably occur when real
objects are given specificity by the hypo-
taxis that characterize poetry's unexpected
formulations.

Boucherie

The freshly slaughtered soldiers are brought in & hung beside the ducks, hooks through their throats, but the shoppers ignore them. Why buy a huge sinewy soldier when there are plenty of succulent ducks that will fit nicely into an oven? It is only at the end of the day, just minutes before closing time, that one of the soldiers is sold, a pudgy sixteen year old to a crippled widow who, because of her infirmities, must be content with the leftovers.

Surprise Attack

Astraddle a helium-filled whale bladder cruising slowly above the coast of Normandy, the begoggled & fur-coated pilot is blissfully unaware of the giant squid rapidly approaching from ten o'clock high.

Executions

Murderers & rapists are thrown from the windows of skyscrapers in these events, which now occur daily, spectators often crushed by these falling bodies. Is the saying *two birds with one stone* applicable here? Probably not.

Money

It's in a ditch.
So what if they get dirty – get your hands on it.
Stuff your pockets full, then up & out.
That now, on high with it, you might look down
                    from whence it came & not get dirty.
That now along a ridge you'll have the wherewithal
        to dance a rich man's jig with nothing spilling over.
Hand in hand with others like yourself & nothing ever lost.
For all of eternity with others like yourself – this
                merry dance that those with money do.

A Pilgrim's Progress

1
Who on a path that only to a market leads is but
a frilly man who once upon he thought he heard
the tinkle of a lost drummer

is not my concern.
Am only on this cart for my health.
Am only going thus for a gourmet's song.

For glass on this path, & in the wayside beds
a bleeding host of questing men who barefoot
in a breach had thought to run & win. But patience

is mine, as it must be – this heavy cart with its limb
from limb load of a once magnificent ox that on
spindly legs a golden calf is pulling.

2
In a stone chair in a stone forest
is a trading man who trading a hound
had only meant to cut his hair.

Which is why he is here.
Which is why he is frozen here watching
a man like himself who wherever he goes he goes

on an ice floe. For to him, the one
who easily everywhere goes, the thought
of a cut hare is repugnant, is not

a fit subject for a song upon
a monumental chair. O glorious the going
of this other who before he sinks will truly sing.

About Blue

What to sound was what I was told to do.
Can you hear it, the blue in this mouth?
It reminds me of one of my crawls for.
It was in water but it couldn't keep me.
For this – to be kept by water, I was not born.
In which not buried, even if holy, this wet.
Not down to the sea in a body (& once is never enough).
That elsewhere the lines are blue & also available.
So why not use them for some accomplishment
About which, this other blue, a bird is not confused?
But removed, trimmed down, what's left? Wings, a pair?
And twice removed? One, one only, & for which
                    this word – wing – it will not be divided.
Alas, the slow process of removing it, this word,
                                            from my body
That another, of some other color, might be heard.
And to arrive with that, with a red, or with a white.
O red & white (& blue) – o say if you can still see
How proud I am on my knees, that conclusion.
And the other, to a market, sold.
A mouth with a price, spoken.
What to sound – what I was told.
One of my words for, but I would not be reminded
It was in air & it kept me.

Exile

Before, when we lived in a room with no blown horse, flies
as thick as a whoop, we were as clear
as clear can be in our red
rubber hats. Seven
seats we had for to keep
our seven mothers neat, & when they were gone
that we'd have seven more we knew
for a fact & the other fact was: blessed be
the medicine dabblers (whose constant menace
kept us warm). What harm

was there in that? Plenty,
they must have thought, who drove us out
with a yawn. But howl
about that? – who would
have listened? So sequentially
is the way we've been, spooning
what we can & in general pulling no face
at the interrogators who thrice weekly are sent
to ply us, song
their only excuse. Abuse (we know it
when we hear it) about jolly
up, niggle fingers, playback furies, astonish
giggles, meat-pie dupes, dim duplicities… in
& out it goes, & up
& down, & around & around, & it won't
ever stop unless… somehow, somewhere
another room (o miracle
of miracles) as cozy
as our first – blown horse, flies
as thick as a whoop.

My Glance

I made my glance. It was
at a radio & it meant
that I had a dog to slay on a casual
basis, a lazy no-frills slaughter
that I could take my time over & if
done pretty enough there'd be a mile
of fishing to hire through
a corridor &, who knows, might catch
a Full Beauty & then – Ample! Full! As big
on the flesh as I can get & all because
I'd made my glance. It was
at a radio & it meant that with
a dog dead I could sit at my table
& eat my fill without a care
in the world, no concern
for the skin on the teeth
of the ones I'd hung & all because
I'd made my glance. It was
at a radio & it meant that although
it's always been my wont to declare
that on the underside of the beast only
is the burden to be found that I'd need
to change my point of view – belly
up & give no thought to the movements of this
or any feast & all because
I'd made my glance. It was
at a radio & it meant that if
I was going to be loved in all
my parts & whole I'd better
change their names & do it quickly, from

Samantha to Sheridan, from Robyn
to Royce & so forth & get them out
where they could hear them before
they took their hunger somewhere
else, my lovers in
their tens of thousands – on
the radio.

Colonels

Pudding is their proof.
Look to heaven for their laundry.
Into girdles are squeezed by acolytes.
Are groomed in kennels.
Are meticulous with nostrils.
Carry buckets for to quaff.
Are at their best in pantries.
Wear bibs for sex.
Have gladiola manners.
Give vent to the patter of paterfamilias
Are pleased when camels kneel.
Will privilege a goat if it's plural.
Tread lightly in animal areas.
Take turns clicking heels.
Assume positions that presuppose a gap in the populace.
Have been known to jerk a few.
Think twice about a sofa plunge.
Percolate with plucked courage.
Are permeated with pathos.
Make feints with emulsions.
Make light of glaring contradictions.
Make goggle eyes at Outraged Innocence.
In kind have met the meek.
Will always argue that less is more.
Have more options than sticks can shake at.
Assemble for trenchant farewells.
Never take a curtain call.
Are resurrected as a matter of course.

Howard

His is an evacuated face. Actually, it's an extrajudicial
face permeated with *suck this immunity* as a function of
fraternal arcanum. In other words, it's a face of
extortion modified to suit the present political climate –
slapdash. Or, to put it simply, an about face. A packed-
with-lies face. A floundering in malignancy face. An
orchestrated by the lowest common denominator face.
A scrummed face. A face, in the final analysis, that's
down on all fours.

A Matter of Speculation

How much
did they weigh, in total, in
pounds, naked, the dead
while alive?

A Concert

As the flautist
Only has one eye the crow
As though on a branch can perch
On the flute & not be heard.

Ivan & Alexandria

Ivan pulls up
A female dress
& makes women's water.

Alexandria unzips
Male pants
& makes men's water.

Correspondence

Home to find the party in full swing. Complete
strangers. Ordinary looking people, but something's
missing – no drinks, no food. *Their nourishment
comes from elsewhere.* "It's nothing
to be concerned about," she says as she leads me
into another room, my bedroom, where she shows me
the capsule that she keeps under her tongue. Could
it be cyanide? Bite at your peril. I've lost
my appetite. Which is just as well because the party's
over, the last guest leaving with my children
in tow. I'd like to go too but don't have a ticket,
turned away by the conductor, the locomotive hissing
in the moonlight as its huge wheels slowly, reluctantly
begin to turn, my garden
ground to a pulp. *Their nourishment
comes from elsewhere.* From
Constantinople possibly. "Your children
will like it there." Waving
from a window (Victorian children
in an ornate frame) they promise to write.

Getting Clean

Filthy because first, I fell from a family
of fifty. No explanation save Fusion, that it fed
the lilies with death until time
became thin, brittle, expired in a long, pathetic
stouche. *Stouche*: run aground – blue canoes (why
blue? – an antidote to the narrator's filth?) are picked up
by painted warriors & carried into a dense forest, never
to be seen again, a gratuitous image whose only purpose
apparently is to disrupt the flow
of the narrative. *Stouche*: how long
can a breath last? Eighty seconds? Ample time
to let them pass. How many were there? Too many
to count. Mares or stallions? Couldn't tell
with all the dust. Should I make them blind, add
an unnecessary complication to a narrative
already burdened with one superfluous image (blue
canoes)*? Stouche*: a stampede
into a feast where the rationing is exceptionally
strict that sends them flying as befits a narrative
that extols the pieta-like austerity of a mother & son
huddled together on a drifting raft (Niagara thundering
in the distance) who can't get over the fact that the tombs
(with which both shores are lined) are so… prophetic, so
stouche as prayers for salvation are answered only
to run afoul of the Law. Too supernatural, this
phenomenon, there could be a panic. Clear the court
of spectators! (&, by extension, the streets of filth
with a water cannon). *Stouche*: clean
because last, the narrative reduced (by a neat
solipsism) to the narrator, that family of fifty
of no further use.

Law

.........for Genevieve

In accordance
with the Law of Stone:
behind each tree
the tongue is a child.

In keeping
with the Law of Opposites:
under water it's wind
that writes the book.

As stated
by the Law of Spoons:
stir blood until it thickens
into speech

Conforming
to the Law of Distance:
skin must stretch
from A to Z.

In compliance
with the Law of Numbers:
each body must add
its spoke to the wheel.

As decreed
by the Law of Silence:
like paratroopers in trees
we're left to ponder what we've heard.

An Incident in Famagusta

First, on a real table
a real pie, sliced (no way of knowing
how it got there). And then, as though
the two events were connected,
we found her in a bath bleeding
from both wrists. Too late, obviously,
to save her. Why? Because outside, in the canal,
a barge with her name – Margaret – on its stern
was passing under a bridge. It was being poled
by a man who was probably naked, naked
because it seemed that he should be (the mist
too thick to see if, in reality, he was). But what
we did know with complete certainty was that
the water in the canal had stopped flowing. It
was simply waiting. For the Moor
was overheard to say: *Pure Christo polls high
in the Famagusta District,* which was obviously
where we were for where else would water, in sympathy
with a suicide, stop flowing? And wouldn't start again
until life resumed its normal course, i.e., until those
who discovered the body (the *we* in this narrative)
called the authorities, etc. &, incidentally, opened
the window that faced the canal & shooed out
the hundred or so birds that had been crashing
against the walls & windows of the little *chamber of horrors*
where she chose to end her days. Birds that, by rights,
should have been in a pie.

Chassé

Ceausescu left laughing
Try charming harder
The platinum gag was my idea
At which point the hunting simply hums
A hymn in praise of human pelts
Try charming harder
Sing out what your price is
Sorry not to have heard your giggle, was otherwise engaged
If you have any Christians it's time to listen to them closely
It was mine – that little fascist intuition
From literal mud he crawled to run with literal dogs in
The time it takes to tow a mother
Hooded emissaries bring out their tubas for a blow
At which point the hunting starts to complain
About those tidewater gadgets that weren't reported in prayer
Meeting sheep with brutality – give it a try
While they twitch your guilt
Is pleasured, is more than you can bear
The aluminium earplugs were my idea
At which point the hunting simply spreads
The Cantonese until their dead are as supple as ours
Who still insist on budget sorrows
Even though they know as well as we do
That hence to whence isn't really twice as much
The diamond-studded blindfold was my idea.

Bytes

As you would suspect the plow
of infidelity if the ox
had a human face so you would
the dead if they rehearsed their marriages
with wooden spoons (& we won't
insult your intelligence with an explanation
as to why). Suffice it to say
that at this point the metaphor
is already so mannered that its collapse
is inevitable,
           thus, a decline
that could be likened to the sudden change
of a ECG's recorded pulse into a final, straight
blue line, which blue is precisely the blue
of the eyes of the SS Oberfuhrer who at this point
marches in to read a proclamation concerning
the nature of the poetry that will be acceptable
to the Fourth Reich, something to the effect
that it must be clear & concise, easily swallowed
between commercials as you congratulate yourself
on the ever-increasing sensitivity of your palate.

Me, Myself, No Other

It's me, myself, no other who's lying
on this filthy mattress in this hospital
corridor, cloud-sick, humiliated
by their procedures, by the samples
that they've taken
                              &, yes,
it's me, myself, no other who has
but one intention: to make it perfectly clear
that my most ardent wish is to
leave as I came –
on hands & knees, crawling
                              &, yes,
it's yours truly, this humble petitioner
that you see before you who will crawl,
naked, to each in turn, to each
of the mothers, to submit
to their wrath
                    & myself, no
other who will present you, made
with my own hands, of my hair, of dirt
from under my nails, an effigy of myself
to do with as you will
                              & myself, no
other, who's stripped to the waist
in this dim hole, who for twelve hours each night
shovels coal into a boiler – steam
for an engine that must be, can only be
an engine of war

     &, yes, it's
me, no other, who, entering a room
that I thought was empty, finds it full
of steamer trunks & in each, as I lift
its lid, evidence of a failed migration –
a blue snake, hibernating, oblivious
to the intoxication of my flute

         &, yes, it's me
alone, hugging myself, who's crooning
a lullaby as the ox is dismissed, as it sinks
into mist – the ox painted blue
that brought me here cradled
in its horns

    & myself, no
other who, coming among strangers,
can understand their language as if
it was my own, their discourse
of dead horses, of empire, of excrement
& tedium

    & myself, yours
truly, no other, who, at the end
of a long journey, was given a tent
in this camp of cowards, who tonight
around a fire as we warm ourselves,
in gratitude, in terror, will place on the lips
of each of my comrades a kiss
of betrayal.

Talking Trash

Now that John's a big shot in the year 2000
& one, though soon to be terminated
by the man on the mobile talking trash
to a constituency made up of men
exactly like himself – Ethiopianised whites
with a grizzled look although, in reality,
those frowns on those mugs are just
for show. In fact they're incurably optimistic
when it comes down to it, the nitty-gritty
as benign as the honey-coated crunchies
that my three year old daughter insists on having
for breakfast & then we're off
to Little Munchkins (day care center), photos
of deportees nailed to every telegraph pole
from here, Woodford, to there, Springwood.
Piss them off to where they came from. Who cares
if they're burned at the stake or whatever it is
they do to crims in those foreign places. Can't
afford to be concerned about a few reffos when
xenotransplantation risks are spreading epidemic
diseases to the whole of humanity, us included.
And this, of course, is where our man rides in
on a white stallion. *Just keep in mind*
the number of sex & you'll be right
is his advice. *We've already met all but the last*
IMF condition & that one's a piece of cake. With
candles? My daughter's fourth
coming up next week. *Will I die*
on my birthday? She asks on our way
to Munchkins, crunchie stains on her face, slack
father that I am who forgot to wipe them off, always
in too much of a hurry, always off to administer
Erotica Tests to the man on the mobile's hopefuls.
If they scream? Just doing my job.

135

Last Days

If what you say is true – that Auto One
oozes French, slipping its leash
in a video frenzy – then I'm
at a loss to explain why Prime Delux
wasn't prepared to float our tumbles
as shares rising, it should be noted,
by a few points every time the bell rang
which was often the case given the proximity
of St. Michael's. Taken
seriously, our tumbles, they'd ring a posie
that would make the tail-biting principals
of the Dingo Protection Society look like
bank-evicted farmers wielding
cattle prods. Give
it a bash, nothing to lose; at the very worst
a few dingos, as their minders sink
beneath the blows, will slip their collars
& make a beeline for the forest where they'll snap
at the heels of the Three Muses, buck-
naked, as wrinkled as prunes, as they gaze
at their reflections in a black pool. Poor
things, it's no wonder that poetry isn't
what it used to be – the enlightened gossip
of a few disgruntled prophets as, now, around
accidents – Chernobyl, Kosovo, Izmit –
we gather like bees.

Good Work

My dead come up. I brush
the hair out of their eyes,
wipe their noses, give them
a pat on the back & tell them
they're doing well.
You're doing a great job.
It's usually enough
to send them back down
for a week or so.
But not mother.
Up she comes at least
once a day, sometimes twice.
She knows that I know
that she's not doing well
at all, is having a hard time
in fact – my son the hypocrite.
So no pats. *Mother,*
it's simply not good enough.
You'll have to try harder.

Shona Favorites

My Shona favorite is mother still
on her death kick (never
gets enough). If
it wasn't so tarted up
with a death-rattle it could
be the stuff of Kabbala. At least
that's how I see it as I make my way
in her raincoat (two sizes
too small) to Holy Cross by way
of Harare, & how
right they are – for killing, the
killing floors I'm always passing just when a heart
is about to pump its last, some pennywhistle constable
jumping up from behind a bullet-pocked wall
to give me a fright. *If your business is jelly
you'll get no welcome here.* Not me, I'm
on my way to find my Kilroy identity (lost
in the last war) & when I do, Watch out! From
bended knees I'll rise to size, formidable, a patriot
about to turn a healthy profit, the *singularity* there
as heavy as the cage that what's-his-name, Mugabe
carried from village to village until it was full. Two
holes back, who was that? – the little man
who sold me short, & now look at him; he's awake
in a legend, mine, not his, where home sweet home
is home by default. That's what happens
when you live in sex where blood spills. Which
is what his mother did (a curse on her) whose business
was the stuff of jelly.

Grandmothers

Sexing the Comtesse de Heureusement while our four
chain-smoking grandmothers watch from the front row
of an otherwise empty theatre, their witticisms aimed at
the core of a performance that, as always, is interrupted
by Japanese pearl divers with offerings (my urge to deposit
my sperm on their diminutive breasts curtailed
by the grandmothers' strenuous objections) – already
as-if-by-magic strung beads that the Comtesse & I take
turns pushing up & pulling out of one another's anuses,
an exercise that's guaranteed to produce mutual
orgasms to the delight of the grandmothers who, at
those moments, rise as one to stub out their cigarettes
on our writhing bodies.

Soft Targets

Junkies who spank make a difference.
As does Nick Brown in his pee-stained underwear
taking the sun on the fifth floor balcony
of the Miami Hilton. From which something –
séance ectoplasm? – is spilling over into
everyday life, whatever that is, which in any case
unfolds on a sweet-smelling meadow where two
tattooed punks emerge from the cockpit of a biplane
to welcome us aboard. Aboard what? – this world
with its sum total of human bodies? Yuk, thanks
all the same.
          Mama & Papa
if you can't manage a hallelujah in the midst
of this ménage who will?
          On track
if you can, & we're right behind you, right up
to the last interior monologue with its backlog
of sordid realities to sort out – earth
& water skills, if ever they were needed it's now
as we lift our hands to make a difference.

Discipline

for Judith Beveridge

One runs
an earth machine
& one a fire but neither will escape
his discipline – the vulture trainer's.

Saint Vitus sulks, his dance
gone to seed that will not, no matter how
exquisitely cared for, grow
in this ground, his ground –
the vulture trainer's.

Alone at night
under a lamp, asleep
with a book in her lap that he
who has written it, who in fact has written
every book, has come on tiptoe
to inscribe – the vulture trainer

Of what
are they made & are they good –
these oils that we use for slurping
in & out – are questions
for him, for the vulture trainer.

And what does it mean: *An environment
that's comatose with constellations of high-
risk keening?* Again, it's a question
for him, for the vulture trainer.

They seem to be everywhere now — these
collection points for what
in ourselves is obsolete
is what he thrives on —
the vulture trainer.

How adorable the figure
that you've cut & from what
fine cloth. So tell us, now that
it's finished, what cause for death
in one so young: some subtle
trace perhaps, some hint
of his influence? — the vulture trainer's.

Down the aisle, demonic eyes
on either side & then the child,
apparently mischievous, who steps
on her train that torn like flesh
is for him, & him alone —
the vulture trainer.

And here a taste
of what's to come, as though from all
we've yet to eat when we are old
in homes, shivering, fed
through tubes from bags that he
keeps full — the vulture trainer.

And here, like sailors' swaying ghosts
in an underwater hulk, are those
who would not listen as they listen now
to the muffled music that he, through glass,
conducts — the vulture trainer.

The applause,
though feeble,
is from the heart for what
he's filled, as though
from a horn, our vessels with –
the vulture trainer.

Bicycle

It's my fifth birthday & I'm sitting on the present that
Uncle Stan has just given me, a green Schwinn bicycle.
He gives me a push & down I go, down the gentle slope
in his back yard in Chicago that becomes a hill, an
interminably long hill that, sixty years later, I'm still
going down, the bicycle having become rusty &
dilapidated but still capable of moving as fast as the
wind. Fortunately the doors, front & back, of the houses
I'm passing through are open & the corridors
unobstructed, the people, my friends & relatives, in the
rooms on either side of the corridors going about their
business as though I don't exist: Aunt Mary & Uncle
John sitting at opposite ends of a long table, John's
prayer of thanksgiving going on & on while the roast
beef gets cold; Aunt Jane having one of her fits in the
kitchen while Uncle Max looks on helplessly; cousin
Dan & his new bride, Eleanor, banging away on a hide-
away bed while the radio newscaster tells us that
Normandy has just been invaded – D-Day. Over a
hundred houses & I'm still going, Uncle Stan passing
away at the age of ninety-two, the war in Vietnam
grinding to a halt, the Berlin wall torn down brick by
brick as I roll by on the Schwinn wondering how the
hill has managed to descend through seventy two
countries on five continents – a mystery I'll never have
time to fathom because there, at what appears to be the
bottom of the hill, is an open grave, half a dozen people
standing around it as though waiting for a hearse to
arrive.

Lucy

Was told this tale by a Mr. Mustafa Mrabet, a downtime
dealer in potions & fortune who had my ear
on a user pays basis, your basic scam. How, so
the tale went, a certain Lucy of Lune
was sunk in psychosis, up to her nether
in the stuff of candelabra, Virginia Slims
on the rebound from a sanctus fiddle, fleeced pilgrims
fleeced twice, body & soul, by the notorious
Robertson, Jack, Bookmaker to the Nazi scum
in Turnbridge Bell. You rang?
  For Mrabet,
to get on with his tale, Ms Lucy left
in a lurch – a March hare, the shrinks concurred
& prescribed a crusade: send her forth
to destroy the infidel on his own turf – a forest
of needles with eyes to pass through
any way you can: strip down & grease up
as though for a channel swim, every day
D-day at this resort, neo-Nazi thugs on a seaside
holiday, exhausted Lucy probed by Fritz & Karl
as she flops ashore, is hog-tied & taken
to East Berlin, gang-raped for a week, then left for dead
on a back ward.
                This one's chronic. Give her
a chair, a rocker, & some pills – Nembutal lullabies
until she's asleep, the last lamb (a wolf in the guise of)
counted in grandmother's bed. *All the better*
to eat you with, ex-lover Hyde smacking his lips
while Jekyll jams a needle home, a tunnel of love

as black as ink.

         My potions, hissed Mrabet, *come
with a life-time guarantee*, a vial purchased
to shut him up, the tale continued with a twist: it seems
that Lucy's a he, a queen in drag who struts her stuff
on Potsdamerplatz, Reichstag ghosts cum stage-door
dandies with carnivorous bouquets. *All the better…*

                           A candlelit
dinner for two at McDonald's, Mac the Knife
& his entourage of deadbeat junkies begging
for scraps, *a little something*, Mrabet tugging
on my sleeve, *to get you through the night*, the first
of a thousand & one in which they unfold – my story
in Lucy's story in Mrabet's…

Perfection

So much perfection in such a small man. All ten fingers
exactly the same size & shape, any one easily
substituted for any other & always immaculate &
likewise his toes, all exactly the same (you don't
believe me? – check them with these calipers) & the
testicles – perfectly symmetrical & hung at the same
level (again, easily verified) & what he thinks, his
impeccable thoughts, all exactly the same, the same
thought, over & over – O the wonder of so much
perfection in such a small man.

The Authorities

Without arms or legs, they wiggle out of the sea & up onto the beach shouting commands from fish-like mouths, the authorities. "Put your best & bluest eyes in the crinkled scars where our limbs were attached! Hurry up! What are you waiting for? You know the penalty for disobedience." And so, timid creatures that we are, we do. We always do, always hoping that we haven't lost the ability to grow new eyes, bluer & better eyes than the ones we give away.

Lost in the Amazon

The canoe of this admiral (who by some miracle has remained unharmed) is so full of arrows (at least a thousand) that it's bound to sink at any moment, & of course the no-longer-paddling & now saluting admiral is honour-bound to go down with it, a fitting end to a glorious career.

Milk

"Sailors on cattle. And they don't have saddles. What's the world coming to?" "It's coming to the time, & very soon, when everything will be milked for all it's worth: sailors & cattle, ships & seas…"

Traps

Article 12 expressly forbids the digging of traps in public gardens. Article 13, in apparent contradiction to 12, declares that all traps in public gardens must be camouflaged with the leaves of banyan trees, oak leaves never, under any circumstance, to be used for this purpose. Article 14, in apparent contradiction to 12 & 13, states that everyone, without exception, who has fallen into an oak-leaf covered trap in any public garden in the month of May is required to attend a banquet at the Town Hall on June 1, a banquet presided over by the mayor who at this solemn occasion will present keys to the city to the May trapees.

St. Pierre Market

How strange that I'm the only one who's noticed that
all of the beggars gathered at the edge of this market
are mermaids, bare-breasted old women who smell of
the sea, its roar in the conch shell begging bowls
audible apparently only to me.

Refuse

At number seven Rue de Lamark a huge cathedral-like
door is pushed open & out stumbles a boy in rags
struggling to maneuver an old wooden wheelbarrow
that contains the withered body of his grandmother
who, moments later, is unceremoniously dumped down
the steep Rue de Fontaine staircase.

Gold

Hiawatha's Hawaiian executor chooses to disregard the antics of Zania Bryce who, having just rushed into the Café Zamboco to deliver a slap to the face of her suitor, the elegant immigrant Paco Rojas, is now sitting on a curb waiting for the Money Men to cruise slowly by in a black Cadillac. She knows that one of them will open a door & kick out a corpse that will land at her feet, a body worth its weight in gold if only she can manage to drag it into the Body Shop just a few doors down from the Café Zamboco, a task for which she'd like to enlist the services of Paco, but he of course will refuse (he always does) not wanting to soil his elegant immigrant's hands (hence the slap on the face) & so she has no recourse but to approach with a great show of humility Hiawatha's Hawaiian executor who, beneath the hard exterior, is a man of compassion. It's a struggle, but between them they manage to drag the corpse down the footpath & into the Body Shop where, as expected, it's found to be worth its weight in gold.

The Violin

Sick & tired of lying passively on a table gathering dust
while it waits for the child to pick it up & draw from it a
few excruciating groans (is life really that bad?), the
violin contemplates a course of action.

Of the many possibilities, most of them unrealizable
fantasies, it decides on one that is sublime in its
practical simplicity. Meditating on a mandala
(remembered from its lifetime as a Tibetan monk), it
slowly but surely transforms the four pegs in its scroll
to wheels, tiny wheels to be sure but sufficient to
transport it to the four corners of the world, or at least
as far as the conservatory where, hopefully, some
accomplished musician will put it to use, drawing from
it, if not a Vivaldi concert, at least a danceable jig.

Windows

All the better to see with, we take our windows with us
wherever we go. Which isn't always easy. If you've
ever tried to take a window into a cinema or a posh
restaurant or onto a bus or plane you'll know what I
mean. There's always some   busybody,   some
presumptuous maître d or stewardess there in your face
with an objection. A bribe, a small one, is usually
enough to send them packing, but occasionally you
simply won't be let in or on, & it's then that you're
forced to leave your window in a cloak room or cargo
hold & accept the fact that your sight will be temporally
impaired.

Voodoo Realities

get the upper hand, the best of me -
bloated men on a lurching bus[1] getting off
at my stop to follow me home. *Please,*
if you let us tie you up we'll tickle you
until you come. Yes, of course,
why not, nothing to lose
but my life. Interesting
as theatre, but I'll give it a miss. Thanks
anyway. Sleep
is all I need, a few hours to recover
from a very hard day that began at seven
at the Bar du Marche on the Rue de Buci, trying
to read a newspaper but constantly interrupted
by buskers on bicycles fitted out with drum kits & this
on the street where naked Rimbaud in the open window
of Verlaine's third floor apartment entertained
a scandalized crowd for an hour, Madam Verlaine,
beet-red with anger, screaming at Paul: *Get him out*
of my home, now! Now! Are these buskers
inspired by Rimbaud? Probably not. And then,
at one, encircled under the Eiffel by those Indian touts
jingling those rings of miniature Eiffels
like keys to paradise, Custer's last stand, fingers
in my ears. I can still hear them. Or perhaps
I've come down with a case of tinnitus. *Could*
it come to this? was the question I asked (on the corner
of the Avenues Foch & Malakoff) a gendarme
in reasonably good French. Arrogant bastard,
he gave me that stupid tourist look & shrugged, obviously
not seeing that herd of sheep with swastikas carefully

155

sheared on their sides² that was making its way down
Malakoff, heading home from the Bois
de Bologne. I followed them as far
as the Place Charrles de Gaule where, passing
under the Arc de Triomphe, they vanished
into thin air. Or had I momentarily been blinded
by the setting sun? Best, I thought, to give up
& go home too, jumping on that bus that took
four hours to reach my destination, bloated men
getting on at every stop.

1. an image from a dream recounted in Jung's *Man & His Symbols*
2. an image from a drawing by Chris Hipkiss

Houses

Gurdjieff's
Guthouse. Green. It's
for rent. Eighty-five cents
per minute. The proprietor: a monk
in combination. On your knees. In
your mouth – given to suck – both barrels
of a sawn-off shotgun. Exit to
Blavatsky's
Bughouse. Blue. Seventy-two cents
per minute. The proprietor; a monk
in lieu. On their way
to the operating theatre – grinning patients
on trolleys. What's so funny? Ether's
exit to
Huxley's
Hexhouse. Yellow. Sixty-one
per minute. The proprietor: a monk
loaded, cocked. A corridor
of stately elms. In their tops, in nests – junkies,
just-hatched, hungry. Exit to
Koestler's
Krankenhouse. Red. Fifty-eight
per. The proprietor: a monk
ticking. Thrown overboard, passengers
applauding, just part of the show
which must go on. Exit to
Freud's
Fuguehouse. Orange. Forty-
three. The proprietor: a monk
as string, thrummed. Orange wig
& withered thighs. He's yours

for nothing, his taste like a penny
under your tongue. Exit to
                              Jung's
Jousthouse. Silver. Thirty-
six. The proprietor: a monk
by monks spent. Children
scavenging corpses. They won't
be shooed away. No
respect. Exit to:
                         Reich's
Ribhouse. White. Twenty-
nine. The proprietor: a monk
cancelled. Paper & pen, ready
to have the last say, the pen ever
so gently removed from your fingers
by a smiling nurse. It's time
for bed. Sweet dreams.

Party

Bring your favourite corpse to the party.
Fun & games for everyone.

I take mother.

Egg & spoon: mother in a swoon,
I shuffle to the finish line.

Pin the tail: blindfolded & spun around three times,
I pin it to mother's stomach.

Fox & geese: foxy lady, I'm the goose again.

Tag: levitating, she can't be caught.

Treasure hunt: mother the treasure,
she can't be found.

Parcel-parcel: unwrap my prize, she's it.

Three-legged race: legs tied together,
we finish last.

Brothers

Home alone, late at night, doing what I always do. I'm rowing. Sitting on my kitchen chair, chained to an oar, I'm one of a hundred slaves making sure that the galley keeps moving forward through a sea that is sometimes calm, sometimes raging. Forward, to that distant port where, so rumor has it, we'll be set free, at long last, after all these years. The others, my brothers in chains, sitting in chairs in their own kitchens in this huge sprawl of public housing, rowing ceaselessly, with a strength they didn't know they possessed.

How much further? How many more days? It can't be far. But what if I'm the only one who's still rowing (the galley seems to have slowed down), the others simply sitting at their kitchen tables guzzling beer, munching on pretzels? Those lazy bloated pigs, of course they've stopped rowing. They've left it up to me. Some unspoken agreement among them to stop rowing. *That fool in 108, he's still flogging himself; he's insatiable.*

Asylum Nerves

Pretend more than ever
that you're being nursed
by a motorcycle mama
with a six-day beard & plenty of time
for a bad case of asylum nerves – neuron
maze, dogged
at every step by thugs who aspire to something more
than pocket-money; you're
just another number to crunch
as far as they're concerned, the volume turned up
while they do it, Beethoven's
Battle Symphony, how appropriate.
                                How long
can you last? – these incursions into the stuff
that makes you you; it's surely
women's business this, & it's done
by men to music while ex-Ranger
Daniel Devine demonstrates his 'Nam pig-sticker
to the girls next door.
                        How
exciting, already bored with you,
your tormentors wander off to have a play
with that giggling entourage.
                            Your you,
it seems you can keep it, a mother's milk
to soothe your nerves.

Books

As the only naked white man in our village
who could cook a book with a single match
it's up to me (my lot in life)
to get the word out where it can be seen
for what it is – pharmakoi. For example,
if you took all of the men by the hand
who have taken you by the leg & led them
up George Street to the intersection where
Rachael's grandmother has set up her treadle-
driven Singer sewing machine, the train
of Rachael's wedding dress hopelessly snarled
in rush-hour traffic, irate motorists on mobile phones
demanding retribution while meter maids nonchalantly
collage their windscreens with parking tickets
(Schwitters would love it) you'd have enough (men)
at that wedding rehearsal to successfully invade
six or seven of those no-name places
that continually export their ne'er-do-wells
to our fair land – pharmakoi – scapegoats who,
dressed to kill in St. Vini hand-me-downs,
in addition to seducing our wives & daughters
have taken our jobs as well, such as they were,
in my case a cooker of books.

The Angel

She came for sex
& stayed
for menopause

at which time her wings
got crisp like a moth's
at a candle, although,

as far as I can remember,
there were never any candles
in our house, that romantic gush

not kosher at our basic-
as-ballast meals, the angel
chowing down with my wife & I

as if she'd just been released
from some horrible camp somewhere,
food dribbling on her white smock

or whatever it was she always wore
even in bed, lying between us furiously,
famously masturbating, our offers of assistance

rejected unless for three days running we'd
not indulged in our thrice-weekly knock-down-
&-drag-out brawls in which she'd usually

intervene, now taking my side, now
my wife's, the subtly of her arguments
invariably leaving us both dumbfounded

which was probably her intention
in any case. "Now let us kneel
together & pray," she'd always say

in conclusion, an exercise in piety
I'd have no part of, going off to sulk
in some corner, & in any case

after twenty years were we any better
for her visitation? Any closer to resolving
our considerable differences? "No,

decidedly not," I said to her on the day
she left, packing her few belongings
in a handkerchief & slipping out

through the back door, taking care
not to brush her charred wings against
the branches of our apple tree as she ascended.

Arthur

At sixty
a long-time resident
of Ward 12.

Catatonic
his record said, implying
stiff, ritualistic movements

which fitted him
to a T, refused
to wear shoes, walked

like a robot, rake-thin, had
to be coaxed, cajoled, driven
down the two flights of steps

to the cafeteria. *Catatonic*
until one day when, a young
idealistic orderly, I was going

around the ward cutting
toenails, Arthur's
as hard & brittle

as old glass, eagle's talons
that curled around & up into
the bottoms of his toes.

Thirty minutes
to chip them off, Arthur,
unnailed, putting

on shoes, going down
to the cafeteria, gaining weight,
no longer *Catatonic*.

Djinns

They come through
loud & clear – speakers on poles
in camps for connoisseurs of liturgical
excess, the last consignment of internees arrested
at Les Girls – priests in drag taking it off
while nuns in mufti worked the crowd. Trained
on rosaries, they could pick the gold from your teeth
before you could say *Jack Robinson*. Jack
Robinson, wasn't he a famous baseball player? That
was Jackie, played with the Dodgers in the late
40s, early 50s, on the cover of Time, celebrated
in song, Most Valuable Player, the djinns
in the crowd grinding their teeth every time he came
up to bat. Obviously he wasn't in their good books,
too self-possessed perhaps. Did he find it
disconcerting? Without those teeth could his average
have been even higher? Grinding like coastal steamers
caught on coral reefs, exotic cargoes spilling
into the crystal clear waters of uncharted bays, only
the occasional connoisseur, having walked away
from one of the many camps for his kind, finding
a chest of teeth – cobra, crocodile, tiger – that
had been washed ashore. They never get very far,
the connoisseurs, before they're rounded up, naked
& hungry, & carried back to the camps on poles
where they're dumped into cages with djinns. Which
explains why there are so many crazies
in the camps, ten days of incessant grinding usually
more than enough to turn even the most diehard
connoisseur into a raving lunatic.

Face

If yours can be substituted for several
you're in business, says my guardian (at my side
like a shadow). But which business? Odds are
that it's dubious. A straw concession, say – selling
straws to those old men kneeling on the riverbank
who love to spend their day sipping muddy water, a
kind of wisdom getting one supposes; or as a vendor
of inflammable pulpits – up in flames as the sermon
comes to a close; or as a shipping magnate – cargoes
of haloes to Sierra Leone, dreadlocks to Outer
Mongolia, ostrich feathers to the Arctic, the ship
crashing through ice, a child's frozen hand
pointing the way to a village where bicycles
are adjusted for human use. Ride
at your own risk. Pitfalls more numerous than mouths
in Ethiopia waiting for food that never arrives. Held up,
as always, by the *Authorities,* in this case a clutch
of bellicose elders exposing themselves to confidence
men in the hope that they'll be selected for *cross-*
chilling, a process similar to cross-dressing, the only
significant difference being that the former takes place
on a cross, the gender switch accomplished before
a crowd of thousands. In the words of the Virgin: *Let*
them rise to this solemn occasion even if it's only for
yet another publicity shot, paparazzi circling, cameras
snapping like the teeth of hungry wolves. Which
gives rise to the question – are these elders
on a hunger strike? – the answer
a loud *No,* nor is their constituency back
in that Ethiopia that Mussolini's air force
bombed in '35, Bruno, his pilot son, marvelling

167

at the spectacle, one worthy, surely,
of a Sistine Chapel. Love the way
those bodies fly. God's children
on the move. *Safe journey*
about as applicable as a fly in aspic
in a confessional, the priest & the client
having somehow switched places, the former
gloating over that boy he'd been a fisher of in '42, a
practice known in the trade *as fingering the beads;*
nice work if you can get it, if you don't
blow the cover, the *acoustic plug* which, subject
to explosions of a gaseous nature, has been known
to fly through the air with the greatest of ease, a
truly abominable practice which in no way
reflects upon the morals of those creatures who
supposedly inhabit the mountains of Tibet, belief
in their existence not being a prerequisite for
liberation, obviously, as all phenomena, belief
included, dissolve like mist when the practice
is truly ripe, *your face as a substitute for several.*

Panzer

Thousands of seagulls on the beach at Benghazi, so
many that we literally can't see the sand. Not
what we expected on this quest for one of Rommel's
panzers, even if it's only a burned-out hulk with only
one survivor. Could this be him, this ancient blue-eyed
beggar in rags? He does look German. *Guten Tag.*
But he's wise to our game. He's not about to speak
in German or any language. Have a look
at that begging bowl. It's a tank helmet. Of course
it's him. Which puts me in a very awkward position.
Why? Because I'm living in his flat in Berlin. Of course
his landlady thought he was dead & it's been, how
long? Fifty-seven years. Fifty-seven years, I wonder
what he'd make of the two drag queens who live
next door, that hysterical laughter, that booming Wagner?
Those two, always trying to get me in drag for a night
on the town. What would our silent beggar say
to that? Would he let us ride on the turret
of his panzer? – showing some thigh, V
for Victory as we clatter through villages on our way
to Benghazi, can't see the sky for the gulls.

Great Work If You Can Get It

Sniping. The company provides a tree house equipped
with running water, TV, a bed, a toilet, a refrigerator,
etc., all of the amenities that one might find in a small
apartment. And once a week, usually on a Saturday
when business is slow, an armoured vehicle deposits a
female, a young woman well-trained in the arts of love,
at the base of your tree. Simply drop the rope ladder &
she's yours to do with as you please until the vehicle
returns in the afternoon to take her back to the city. Of
course there's a quota. Saturday exempted, one must
secure a minimum of five trophies per day, with a
bonus of twenty dollars each for six or more. Some
snipers have been known to collect as many as twenty
trophies in a single day. Simple arithmetic tells us that,
apart from their daily wage of one hundred dollars, they
were able to make, before taxes, four hundred dollars
for a single day's work, a huge sum considering that the
average factory worker is lucky to take home that much in a
month. Needless to say, sniping is one of the most sought
after occupations, but the interview is rigorous,
as are the tests. For every one thousand who apply only
one is accepted.

The Elephant

We're having sex (it's never been so good) when the
door opens & three old women file in. You'd think they
might have knocked first. "Keep going, pay no
attention to us," one of them says as they gather around
the bed. Scratching their chins, tugging on their
earlobes, making *hmmm* noises, they carefully
scrutinize our movements for what seems like an hour
but actually is for only two or three minutes, & then:
"Try The Elephant," & one of them moves closer to the
bed. With shaking hands she carefully rearranges our
limbs into The Elephant position & then steps back to
survey her work. "How silly of me; I forgot the trunk,"
she says as she steps forward again to twist my left arm
behind my back, my cupped hand jammed between my
partner's thighs.

Erasmus

at your feast what choice
did the lambs have? Or we
for that matter, forced to attend by the squalor
of our means? An end to it
at the end of a long tunnel where we, so stuffed
with lamb that we can't walk, are being wheeled
on beds by orderlies, are keeping pace
with trotting men with carcasses
on their shoulders, butchers obviously, but on
closer inspection they aren't; they're oil sheiks
on a crash course with Dan Cann, the new
better management guru – hands-on, get a feel
for the common people, & the question is:
who'll get to the future first – one of us
on one of these beds or one of the sheiks? – punters
in bleachers cheering us on, & the winner is…
yours truly, wheeled
to the winner's circle, a wreath
around my neck & a handshake
from the man himself, who knew I'd win,
have made him rich, the prophet Erasmus.

Voices

We gorged get evasive, introduce screams
as hard core, have a whisper among the ribs
of a reefed ship, escape one hearing only
to be seduced by another & pick our scabs & all
for what? To save on lithium? To have an excuse
to tinkle? Do we need one? Who will anyway
& probably on a radiator because we like
to watch it sizzle & in any case are confused
as to what is proper where. For instance, who
else would expect an aviator for lunch,
his feathers slightly ruffled? Or propeller
blades for open slather? – Get stuck in because
they've got it coming, who were always
off to the side like wallflowers, too shy
for a dance with Doolittle, Court Physician
to Emperor Abdullah the Fifth, what
an opportunity missed; once or twice
in a lifetime if you're lucky, & we were, that
slip & slide from marginalia to total corporate
conviction while chasms yawned on either side, secretions
licking at our heels, momentum gathering
like coffins, their makers on the dodge, can't
get our measure, too quick on our feet to the beat
of the Touchwood Trio. But we aren't (touched)
& here for your consideration is evidence for this
seemingly preposterous claim: *Culled*
with six of the best, a test
we couldn't fail given our propensity for
in situ scare mongering, scare personalities

on the walls, re previous, like flowers
to pluck – thirrrp – from their places
in the scheme of things, which brings us
to the case in point (stated as diplomatically
as possible): *About those knuckles*
of yours, Jimmy, they're just too much
on the hoodoo circuit; & our advice, asshole, is
to get them off before someone notices, slaps on
a finger fine – incessant drumming on the back
of what once was an individual, animal probably,
but how appropriate if it was human, how acquired
a matter of the most exquisite contemplation as we sit
around a campfire roasting our weenies, six
of the best & on this occasion not a test
we'll fail so studied are we in the art of *sitting in*
for others (obviously you haven't noticed
what we're wearing: vintage flying suits, goggles
& helmets, circa 1918, hot on the tail
of the Red Baron who is about to go down
in flames, not, of course, a recommended way
of procuring skin for a drum as the cure
is more sizzle than smoke) *for others* until
the system clears its throat & spits us out
cured ourselves, or so it would seem to the authorities
who are masters at not noticing – that no sooner
are they picked off than we're seduced
by the next hearing.

Halt

They said: "Be sown, it's your duty," but I couldn't
        be bothered; I knew
that I had to hurry – that vial of angel's blood
        to the shrink before
Barnabas got out his old 45 & started playing
        that one about Pity, how
fishing got confused with surgery, or something
        like that, when Alexander
went down for congress with runners (escapees
        from a camp) through
a forest – moonlight, dogs, dead leaves – look
        into my eyes, how
deep they are as I pull the trigger – out alive
        (of course I have a price)
on a cash basis & released into a room that the
inhabitants call *Quits*. Why
do I know this, what the room is called? Because
        a little bird told me
so. Just joking. I know it because Peter Pirozzi
        got up from his stool
& whispered it into my ear as soon as I arrived.
        Which was good (to know
the name of this room) because every would-be
occupant is quizzed by the man
himself, Quits Smith, who's responsible not only
        for its existence but
for its many amenities as well – stuffed animals
        on which to ride (though
they only move in circles as though on a merry-go-
        round you'll get somewhere;

you'll find yourself where you need to be) & dildos
        of every size, shape
& color with which to pleasure yourself during
the interminably long
hot nights in this part of the world &, most
importantly, a full refrigerator. Notice
how it glows in the dark & how it's approached –
with humility, on your knees, a
green cloth bag held open before you into which, if
you're seen as sufficiently
humble, morsels will be dropped from tweezers,
Smith's daughter Juno doing
the honours; or else (insufficient humility) it's back
        to that forest, that rough
voice shouting *Halt*, those executioner's eyes
into which you'll dive for coins. Here's
one, a genuine piece of eight, plunder from the Main,
        worth a fortune but try to use it
in a phone booth, a call to Vixens, to ask about
the rates, just what the doctor ordered –
a long session with a qualified therapist. "What
does he mean: *Clan husks, a pearl
in each?*" "He means leave it cut so you'll know
it's school. He means burning tyres
in hotel lobbies, bargain-hunters blacking-out
on zigzag railways. He means
Business As Usual: polite interrogations – if you
confess to sailor's work we'll provide,
no strings attached, a pot to piss in, end of rainbow
stuff this, if you see it
that way, & why not? – in the end the whole kit &
caboodle is in the eye, obviously, of
the beholder, yours a bit jaded but not irredeemable.
"Be sown," they said, "it's
a chance, your last." So I did. I dropped the vial.

Kif

The tale thus far: sex text
meant licks in a language
I couldn't read. It meant a stop just short
(by a mile) of a rag to fly at the stern

of a rusty tramp freighter riding at anchor
in the Bay of Pigs, my twelve year old dream:
to be a stoker on it, off to see the world
by any means. O love of my life, I couldn't find you

in Shanghai so I looked in Casablanca. But Bogart
got there first, my consolation – an invitation from Ahmed
to smoke some happiness in a green-walled

kif den where Peter Pan flew to an imperial Rome
teeming with sex slaves from the steppes of Russia
& beyond; no stop short, I could read every word.

Cage

Another stick fight
& the winner is… Elaine, the very same
who made a big yellow mess & wouldn't
clean it up. Gave her a mop & a pail

but she wouldn't. Gave her a toothbrush, down
on her knees to scrub, but she wouldn't. Slapped
her silly but she wouldn't? Is she
my mother? Is she your sister? If she is

I won't own up to it. You'd better not
either. Trouble if we do. They'll stop us
from taking the elevator up to Cairo. They'll

drag us screaming from the escalator
to Istanbul. *No pass for a month!* they'll shout
as they shove us in with Elaine.

Cattle

Big wise cattle don't
jell. Does hunting? If
you could tell me what I purportedly
did away with I might possibly

own it. Be rid at last of this
female persona – corset snipped off, manly
chest exposed, etc. But, wait, is this
what I want, this macho image? No, better

back off from it & come at them, the cattle,
from a more compassionate angle, make them
women's business: Dear ladies, it

would please me immensely if we in corsets
penitentially tight could kneel together & give thanks
for the wisdom of cattle.

River

To the tell of a river
is what I wake to. For weeks now
I've been wanting to use the image
of a camel caravan with a corpse
in every pannier. Which I've
just done (who the dead are & where
they're being taken of no consequence). Will
an almightily-conceived image such as the above
become prophecy, realizable in the everyday world?
We'll have to wait & see. Meanwhile
from pillar to post Lawrence is running
amok because he's upset: the wig
that he'd *like* to wear is the wig
that I *am* wearing because, obviously,
I'm the most deserving (if not the prettiest). In
actual fact we, Lawrence & I, are simply two men
who each day scrape together a pile, sometimes
large, sometimes small, & say, look,
isn't it marvellous what we've done! & lived
(no caravan on the horizon) to tell the tale
that the river tells, or seems to,
when I wake to it.

Saint Philip's Infirmary

Are we here to save our lives? Big
should we beg? If we pay enough
can we crawl under? Do our keepers know what it's like
to burn bare naked? With our persons
should they have their fun free? Are they & they
our destiny? Our heroes
to look up to, do they know we know
where the cowards are?
       As always
they're in behind the others. In, just there,
that swoon bordello with the cowboy classic
repertoire: On hands & knees
do Arch of Submission. Or suffer
spurs, some egg on
a face you thought was yours.
        Is time,
little miss, to jump as queen, as promised
to the people. And you too, little mister, is time
to jump as queen as well. Over which if high enough
some good might come: a roll-up single bed, a hi-fi
porno of our very own that every father might
in scratchy song wish us well. Do them proud
& over to Efendi's they may not
today cross us. And possibly won't on us
this morning the glory grabbers sick with terms
of endearment in minor key if ear-trumpets
we've stupidly left in our ears.
        Told, again,
what we already know: In us is folly

fully engaged for which, if we're smart
& know the rules, we'll kneel & do the praise
we've been trained to do by betters. And told,
again, lest we forget, how among the dead
of all the dead we are, by a mile, the most dead.
Flung like stones, all of us.

Wig Hat On

How can I my hatchet with
if too close to a doctor you stick?
Everyone with my good face
gone a mile to mother who to women

always said: Music
might have the time to
but I don't. I'm not among
those lucky few who are dress people, their shame

passed down (transferred) to those who demand
a keeper because they've got
a zoo to feed. A big zoo, as big
as the world. Why not feed

a human child instead? Go ahead,
take my milk money; plenty more
where that came from. To glory I'll come
in any case. My path

isn't walking; it's running to…
…to my death with the help
of that déjà vu contraption I stupidly
put in motion, a moving walkway

at that too familiar airport – Babel
International. This baggage
is unattended. Touch it! Give voice
to a scream. Any minute now

we're all dead. Or wake up
to the shudder of a tram passing through
our pretty pink bedroom, its passengers blind
to the pathetic tangle of our vein-

knotted legs. If only
I could get one up. Wouldn't that be something
to write home about? – with
trembling hands mother opening

my first letter since her death. What's
he up to now? – more words
in yet another book. God knows
to what purpose. Doing well

if he sells three. Fools
with money to burn. Ok, a big mistake
I confess to: *Only one thing I did wrong* –
stayed in Oz thirty years too long. Gotten out

while the getting was good, might have avoided
this infernal machine, its instrument changed
but not the writing, a big time singer
who could with a hatchet do.

As I'm Led Away

As I'm led away
I'm given an instrument to play
& though I've never played
an instrument before
I play this one so perfectly
that children follow me to a river.

As I'm led away
the small frightened animals
that make up my body keep scampering off
to hide & then, missing their brothers & sisters, creep
back again, again become a whole body
that is apparently mine.

As I'm led away
I hear as though spoken through stone
my father from the tribe of Bachelor
ask my mother from the tribe of Virgin
for her hand in marriage & she answers
as though through water, Yes.

As I'm led away
the memories I call my own
fade & others, like lamp wicks being turned up,
take their places. It's thus
that I remember my life as a dervish in Khartoum,
as a merchant in Shanghai...

As I'm led away
the cities where I've lived
topple like blocks
knocked over by children, & the rivers
that run through them dry up
like blood soaked up by rags.

As I'm led away
I begin to understand
that my death is necessary, that
the executioner is a kindly old man
who is wrapping a gift for a child to find
under a tree on Christmas morning.

Kamikaze

Can swallowed pride make up for the loss (by
theft) of my collection of bicycle bells? Probably
not unless those fairy lights in the forest (another
unwarranted hallucination) are extinguished before

my mother, God bless her, deems it an act of charity
to take the downed pilot to church in a wheelchair
as a consolation prize & only because I'm refusing
to go. I will, mother, I'll go. I'll swallow my pride

& go even if I have to cut a swath through the forest
to get there & discover in the process that the fairy lights
are in fact the twinkling eyes of the Japanese pilots

who have crashed & survived, God knows how,
& bring them with me, a procession of suicidal maniacs
on bicycles, bells ringing get out of our way.

France

Charlie Chaplin went to Dance
to teach the ladies how to france. How to chance
was not included in the curriculum. A shame
because here I am stuck in a pint-sized lift

in Paris with Martine & her brain-damaged triplets
screaming blue murder in a futile exercise to invoke
the blue yonder that we won't see again until God
knows when & I don't know what to do. Borrow

Mallarme's dice & throw them – snake eyes
& we'll be rescued by the pompiers in just
two more minutes? If Charlie here would he

know what to do? Have a cheek to cheek
with Martine while I gag the brats?
Sounds like a good plan to me.

Bride to Be

Sick with cough & counter-cough
how to rise from this bed to feel
my bride to be – my
clammy hands – who, in any case,

is already, this bride, the mother
of nine men? Brothers
to a man, all eight
around my bed to wish me a speedy

recovery that I might do
what I'm expected to do with a more
savory someone than this bride

who now, touched to the quick,
has fled my bed,
is refusing to be.

Baby Love

What next? Should I sit by a river
& sell my clothes, a penny each? Would that
make the bathers happy? But what
if it's all about how

you do violet or, worse,
orange? O cat of nine
in a tree of three as into marshland armed
parachutists settle into an unfathomable

melancholy. Is this really what my baby love
for high blue places has come to? Is it time to feel
the death of me? You will of course, on that

I can count, a heartfelt sob & a wave
as my funeral bark drifts
out into the Bolivian Sea.

Ancestors

after Vasko Popa

My great great grandfather David Caspar Nimitz
went fishing with a bicycle chain. Six times
he caught a wife. Five times he let her go.

My great great grandmother Yelena Pavlovna Feodorovich
never told her husband that he owed his success as a father
to the femur of a Siberian she-wolf.

My great grandfather James Jacob Waddell
tied a string to his penis from which, swung
like a pendulum, the world kept time.

My great grandmother Maria Teresa Carbone
measured the world on her knees. Six mile across,
it was as flat as a pancake. Saturated with molasses,
it rotted her husband's teeth.

My grandfather Karl Heinrich Graun
returned from the Great War with a hole in his stomach
from which he extracted a fully operational three-ring
circus. Missing, sad to say, was the man shot from a cannon.

My grandmother Alice Stone Blackwell
tickled her husband's fancy with a cat's tongue,
a rasping from which he never recovered.

My father John Charles Keane
would never sit in a chair because
he was convinced that chairs were the source
of all evil. Why he had no scruples about standing
on chairs has never been explained.

My mother Mary Margaret Church
married a man from the milk horse tribe. As meek
as teeth, he was a man of one word – *No* –
which he kept.

My daughter Genevieve Aloka Welch-Hammial
has ten thousand keys which she keeps in a box
under her bed, one of which, if she can find it,
will unlock the world.

The Entire Lights in Green

Thirteen letters. His name
is on a fence. This man
is your best friend. You'll never
see him again. He won't get up

at the count of ten. Obviously
the death of money
has changed nothing. If that's my flag
you're flying you can kiss my

mom, just a peck. If you'll give me a chance
I'll explain my shoes. At running
I'm not the dull original
you take me for. My reputation made

in a snack bar, did my book
brag? Of course not. Story time
for little lambs? You must
be joking. They're already

shooting us up to here & they've only
just started. Under glass, are we
the new saints? Signed up
for a nature course & now they tell us

it's been cancelled – insufficient
numbers. That excuse might have worked back
in the infancy of antiquity, but now… Now,
in Berlin, surrounded by whispers of a Biblical

nature, we're feeling quaint with a touch
of bold, not quite enough to sing in our chairs
but we're getting there. Possibly on Tuesday
next we'll do our worst (which, as you know,

is our best). Up on our feet, we'll be thirteen
to the dozen, our ovens cum coffers overflowing
like manna into a community of like-minded
bipeds doing their business with Ps & Qs

from which there's no escape if your choice
is to stay in this world. Speaking of which,
is it true that you're being paid
to count the dead?

History

Unmoved (unmanned?) by a moving text
that acknowledges Dame Nell's contribution
to intervention – in clans, blood lust, paddlers up
excremental creeks – I'm putting the finishing touches

to my analysis of boxer rebellions, my contention
that they invariably perpetrate the status quo
given credence by the testimonies of ten Tungus
shamans who should know because they were there

in spirit if not in body. Forget the footnotes & change
your socks. Encrusted with mud (haven't you noticed?)
from your last trip to the Black Lagoon, they reek

like the footnotes to Everyman's History, that hullabaloo
in which, like it or not, Dame Nell is a major player, her
notorious interventions underwriting the status quo.

Hunger

When I listen it hurts here.
Never again will I eat what I cook.
I'm an artist & this is my show.
When it's on I like it large.

That money you spent was mine.
It's a pile for a spoon. Please
dig in. Please give me this day
the actual words of what I say.

On that wall, look, it's my face.
When it's off I like it small.
When I speak it hurts here.

Just a stuffed frock.
Of course I'm in it for me
I'm watching to see what I want.

Bell

I went down where the bell was.
At a long table there were monks bent over bowls.
They were slurping soup.
Disgusting. When, I asked,
  will you stop to ring?
And one, the eldest, wiping his mouth on the sleeve
  of his cassock, replied: The sound that will carry
  your mother home, how big must it be?
It was a good question, & one to which
  I had no answer.
They offered soup, which I reluctantly accepted,
  a bowl, apparently, without a bottom.
When you've finished, said the old monk, I'll make
  the sound that carries your mother home.

A Gigolo from Gilgamesh

'Twas a pocket affair, a pulse
in a deep pocket. That went like this:
she wouldn't worthy me, neither lock
nor stock nor barrel, which, rolling,
would surely have taken us
to some arousal, however
short & sweet, etc. Exit
then? Hop in my new Merc (new
in '49) & be off for some truly
virgin experience, some rush
to circumstance, pomp
with its brown eye blinking?
                              Hold
tight, here I go, crank
on hurdy-gurdy, turn to catch
some lovely if I can. It could
be you or, better, your sister with whom
I had some dealings with in '48. Of
the sick kind: notch a way up until sane
can't be rendered, won't stick
to anything. Cut a deal? Not
with that knife. That senseless monologue
is forever mine. Sister won't
have a bar of it. Exit
then? Safe conduct
from mother love to a spinster sprawled
on a sultan's bed? Why not, it's a bed
I've never been in, a seething Wagon Lit
on the Orient Express to Istanbul where,
knackered, I make a run for it, her
scathing critique of my sexual irrelevancies
like music to my ears.

Mater Tenebrarum

Consider the Chancellor with frocks
in quatrain that plays the fool
for a new skin model might well be
the only three lines in my collected works

worth saving. As for the rest – pain
management on paper as a license
to buzz the Eiffel: how poetic is that? Not
even remotely. "Who goes there?" demands

the dominant male who, like a thief in the thick
of an orchestra, is waiting for Moroccans
with T-bursts. About as likely as four
timpanists on the head of a pin playing

a flawless rendition of that old favorite
Who's on the menu today? Is
flesh contrivance a bowering kind? is a line
not worth saving; as is: Will the bride bored

by her late mother's rebirth as a husband-to-be
be excited to the point of total distraction
by this unforeseen development? Should
we wait, breath bated, to see? Only

if we've got nothing better to do. As for myself,
I need to finish my report on The Bauble before
the lackluster carpet cleaner arrives with another
impossible demand – Deny every number

from one to ten! No way, four as per
the earlier mentioned timpanists is crucial
to my well-being & would be to yours as well
if you had any sense, which obviously

you don't, as testified to by that mother cum
husband you insist on coupling with. "Who
goes there?" "It's only me dragging my pillow
from cradle to grave," that pillow as white

as snow on the armrest of my great grandmother's
still-rocking chair, her house
that fell down around in '37, the year
of my birth, only one door left standing

through which I must pass if I'm going to arrive
at a poem that means something. Fat chance, no chance
at all if they have their say – all of the concierges of Paris
lined up like soldiers on the Champ de Mars.

Biting

The men were biting my arms.
The horse was blindfolded.
No one would extinguish the fire in the next room.
"It will burn forever & you with it,"
   said the old woman, the mother of the men.
She took off her clothes, put them into a box
   & gave it to me.
"Put them on," she said, "& give me yours."
I did as I was told, & became a mother of seven men
   for eight hours.
When I told my sons to bite the old woman's arms
   they refused.
Then we exchanged clothes again.
This went on for seven months.
On the first day of the eighth month the horse was taken
   to the burning room.
After we ate the horse the old woman told her sons
   to bite my arms.

Deathwatch

No, I won't shout out:
Take camel to Captain! Why? Because Captain
already has camel. What about the courage deal?
Has it been done? Yes, to a turn. Wandering
among bonfires on a beach, what's
that foul smell? – a dead
animal. First the ox disappeared
& then the lamb. Throw a knife
into the air, see if one of these fools
is game to catch it. For the price
it's an okay feel, could be better,
could be worse. She turns up with a mule
with two coffins, one tied to each side
of a crude saddle, & shows me
her torn blouse. Who did that? The scum
in the coffins? A deathwatch,
is that what we're doing, what
this poem is about? *Take Easter
to Esther!* (which I'm not about
to shout out). Since when
can an egg break a man? Since Friday
last, those river women
with their insidious narghilehs, smoke
in our eyes, salacious obfuscations
dragging us under. If only you knew
how they rode us (by Jesus approved)
you'd understand why we refuse
to crawl, why we sit on a slope
& mourn the passing of the caravan, camel
to Captain not an option.

Party Animals

Day & night the cattle sing.
It's a most peculiar thing.
And if it's truly so then surely
you'll find at last that place in Heaven, that
woolly cloud from which to help yourself
to fame & fortune. It's there (almost)
within reach.
                    Meanwhile,
in the woods there's a tram
crammed with partying soldiers. Lurching along
like a drunken boat it will soon be stopped
by a mine planted by the anarchist Rigault. To which
tragic event a unicorn & a faun
are the only witnesses, & they
won't tell because they can't. It's a question
of the genesis of the gestalt, or something
like that. Could a workshop
on the Codes of Confession
be helpful here, those atolls of speech
rising & sinking to the rhythm
of a shaman's drum?
                    Meanwhile,
in this poem, somewhere, there's a dead horse
to flog with the proverbial noodle. Clue:
look in the second paragraph; though here
a warning: even if you do find it
you'll never make it sing.
It's a most peculiar thing.

Aeronautics

Pilots fair & pilots steady fly
while I spill you, but who flies
when you spell me? No one,
that's who. Falling fast

as marriage does, it's a tease that does
your gender proud, right proud & might well
be good for life if the death you've found
is the one I lost way back when? – In

forty-one? It's
ninety now & so much easier to ground a fool
who back to back with Sam is back to back

with Sue as well who has the sense
to put them straight, the colors
on a book, the words inside as well.

Hit Parade

Fairy lights on the cover of my latest, what
could I have been thinking of?— that
forty-seven poems about a wrestling match
in foul weather would bring about

a fundamental change
in my star status – from number forty-seven
on the East Anglican hit parade to number one
in one lifetime; how absurd, this poem

a perfect example of my perennial inability
to articulate some universal truth, a sad fact
that's guaranteed to keep me in the ranks

of the also-ran until the day I die or decide
to find some sensible occupation that might take me
to the top; wrestling, with one throw, why not?

Anschluss

Forget the dwarf
who's working his way up from the bottom
of the Zeller See on a rickety ladder & focus
for a moment on Hildegarde who's pushing
at a snail's pace a trolley down the aisle
toward your bed. What's
on it? Let's
have a look: a lyrebird's nest
& in the nest a doll with blue eyes
& jabbed into the doll's stomach
a syringe. It's for you – your morphine: sweet
dreams, your bed a gangplank over which
the Masters swarm as they're piped aboard
the good ship *Palimpsest*. Shipwrecked humanity
a feast for these gods, the leftovers tossed
into a wishing well. Wish
you could get out, but you're here
to stay. It's your very own once-
in-a-lifetime Anschluss. So forget (is my advice)
that divine aspiration & just
hold your breath. The Zeller
is deep, & the ladder precarious.

Prelude

Like Snow White in a heat of kink
I've lost my most. Glad
handles my mouth. Closed
in a cellar situation, I've never had
the satisfaction of cereal. When
I've done a pray I walk away. If
they so wished they could drang me
but haven't yet. If you've done your homework
you know that an axe in kind has half a mind
to. And possibly fro but that depends. It's one
(that one) beyond mistake. So much so that
Shame sends Horn home. Can you recall the issue
of the noise of the skirt he wore? A forced entry
(it says so here) is a commodity that sits 'twixt betrothal
& the next guy. With him we'll never know
if it's dogs or crows. Or a five collar job
in Flute City. Therapeutically loyal,
we're trading blows. Each numbered
as arousal, with eunuchs in attendance. What
in pink cups they bring us to quaff is the same
as that stuff in black cups. Or so we're told. Me? –
collared & caned with no safe word I'd urge
some spill. As all mess eventually must
in this is there too much of us?

Madchin

Jasmund, please, a little help with my head: so terribly
crowded, what shall I do, Dagmar, with that last dog
was I ruined forever, Fani, tell me why Margo
mumbled wish & whey while thinking tea
& stove, Schirin, chicken bread won't do
even though I *am* upstanding, Uta, your faces
all in row which one is really you, Yamina, if ever
a horn becomes a blow I'll be sundered here
& here & here, Heile, sitting on a flashback seat come
& watch me pull, Priszilla, in wretched folly wandering
while for strumpets demons yearn, Yasmin, are
they mine o yes they are all seven thousand
two hundred & forty-six, Sibyl, I'd like to know
if my sweeping up is missed, Maarit, was I accepted
for that U-let scheme, Schontraud, they just me gave
a bucketful of something heavy, Hedda, if it's soup
I won't be having any, Aalina, why with each adherence
a cowardly retreat, Rachel, I'd love to render
a shivering service to someone, Sabinchen, it might
as well be you, Yamina, should I shout to show
my deep, Dyna, should I accept that naked
rider bust, Beate, yes, it was me I was the one
who made the butcher cry, Kathe, this charm
I'm wearing, this head of wolf, what death
will it keep me from, Fadda, if not from some frame
we fell, Fusun, why we killin' each other over
periwinkle, Pancratia, why haggle over trophies
that we with razors won, Wanda, that task you set me –
to plunder the dead – how miserably
I failed, Fatima, this mob in my head, Helga,
how it to out?

Spoilers

At me:
spoilers. They pick up brass,
beat my hair. As I was, beaten,
I'm not now. Is how you find me
& give approval: *Just*
a moll in a squat, on pride
not banking. Time
it was told – how me
& my famous munificence. How I'd picked
to finish: the process as experience
of the author, a working class
growing in Mannheim. Labels there
that spoke as loco – an inner song
of stunned clairvoyance – that were for me
just another look-see: a little man & a large man
pressed together, what they could do
in a bowl embellished with the fiction
of salvation, an extraction
from big jungle writing. At its best
was a dodging to celebrate, legally
& by implication – feluccas & ocelots caught
in crossfire, friendly, while me
I was lathered seemingly for keeps. All fuss
& fury in proud garments rent
like Jesus drawing a picture of God, looks
like nothing so much as treacle & thus how
I came to be as a (second) closet choice
thereby explained: Up with that brass
beating my hair!

Walk That Walk

...don't you think Al Jolson is greater than Jesus?
Zelda Fitzgerald

I do. Doesn't everyone? Machito (Crowded Fingers)
Smith from Shongopovi does. And what about
the Isis mob? *It's a hurt mix.* Any made
in China saints could
(also) be (greater). Although
in the Resurrection Sweepstakes Jolson &
the China saints are long shots (long march
as touchy-feely cattle prod). Me? I'm
only using two fingers to type this &, please note,
my face has wept. In Bolivia duelling
is legal if both parties are registered
blood donors, which in no way accounts
for the wept face, is just some useless information
that adds nothing to the poem. Or does it? – pearls
before swine, these last (four) lines? Legal
duelling, let's to Bolivia. Hey Machito, your fingers
for trigger, you my second, yes? Sheep count
(75) superseded by wolf count (97). It's
Peak Empire as Darling makes her way
to the Ladies'. Walk that Walk
& don't come back empty handed. I won't be denied!
Some Holy Writ at least. My pretty, this army is erectus
& just so you know: Le Nain Rouge is here among us;
you've but to lift your head to see, to look beyond
the Theatre of the Obvious & be damned.

Owls

on the floor, tie strings to their legs, pull
them around. Owls: toys without wheels. One
who blows into the wrong end – of a trombone. One
who blows into the wrong end – of an owl. Two wrongs
make, for owls, a night. Seven brides: they, the keepers
of owls, have dared to suggest that I won't be happy
with less but
six would suffice. What
Attila asked of Nestor at the Battle of San Romano: Why
to owls this show of kindness? Wretched & sumptuous,
a squat among owl-faced clocks. Stubbed out
on flesh: owls clap. Fifty men, fifty women
on twenty-five window ledges: holding hands, two
by two, will jump unless... owls, no
strings attached, jump first. A cheer for Lisbon – owl
chatter silenced. Modus operandi: a flooded forest, oars
for owls. Sailors in trees, coaxed down,
maybe, by... owls. Snuffed
candles: not me who's responsible
for this lack of owl precision. J'accuse: responsible
for my heart attack – that owl perched on my left
pulmonary artery. On the head of a pin: owls jostling
for space. Alone in the mess world (read *hall*): feed
them, now! Cat's bowl: bath
for owls. For Philip the Good: owls
in a game bag. For Philip the Bad: flies
in a game bag. Opening his raincoat, a drenched
dealer in owls. Submissive for a pushing guy, sycophant
as owl surrogate. Common error of owl injection:

sub-temporal orientation. Goth owls: bald with
multiple piercings from which
canaries swing. Mindful of fashion whims, they'd
better be. Perfectly rendered: an owl in wood
to manipulate: obedient marionette. Four corners for
owl blessings, ascertain which is most officious. Quantum
wedges equal (usually) pontifical owls. They
know that we know that they know...

A Bed

This bed, rocking in & of & for itself, it
pleases me immensely. As in (therein) their
not inconsiderable swoons they seem to take &,
occasionally, give delight, by which I mean (& mean
I must) a cautionary cradling for these fornicators who,
unchecked, would intimidate with rocking annoyance
their otherwise willing partners in, if not a serious crime,
a trundling misdemeanor, so that, now, by this (& that)
I'm inclined to say, & kindly so, as gall upon a manner
fixed is mixed & matched as only matter can, an
expression of felicity not
to be fobbed off, no, nor held up
as some so positioned darling pretending ignorance of
a fact basic to yours truly – that aversion
is my hospice although (& nonetheless) if that
is possible (& probably isn't) I must insist
on something, on a something that I've somehow, in
the unravelling of this sentence, forgotten. Speaking
as I was (I remember now) of swoons of
a cradling kind, by which I don't mean anything even
approaching a ravishing, but do (& must) insist upon
a censoring of those who would to a rocking bed take
for the sole purpose of fornication.

Nurse

She's blowing
into my pyjamas. Into my pyjamas
she's blowing & blowing, & a doctor
is hammering. He's
hammering & hammering. My pyjamas
full of nails. On which wall
should I hallucinate a ladder, a nurse
climbing that ladder? Desperate
to escape. From me? The doctor? Not me: tethered
to this bed by a chain, a heavy chain
that she herself attached to my collar (the collar
that identifies me as a Category Three patient). Which
brings me to the question: Why
am I here?
                    I know
why I'm here. I'm here
for Vigilance, a Simple who, for his own safety,
must be constantly monitored. *Who left that window
in that basket?* They did, the padres, the
pushers of glass with knives to cut
the Mexican square from which, again, as always
I'm excluded, left to fend for myself, set upon
by bandidos, a bullet smashing my jaw. It's
floating, my daughter's violin, set free, moving away
from the room where the game-bags are kept. *Who left
that dog chained to a post? Who's sewing it, what's left
of it, into my skin?* – my skin of glass (for vigilance) into
which a nurse is blowing, & a doctor is hammering.

Duffer

with a nurse mania, his goof partner a morass
of disconnect. What a tease! – a snatch tendered
by bandstand silence.
                         Do more fingers
equal more rings? Can sour milk
sustain? Appraised of his grace

he stumbled. Was it a case
of lamp fright? Serious pills,
is that why he did it

with Jack? With Jill? On
a hill that if you rolled down
you'd traffic in feathers

& tar, that white trash queen
a sheriff's wife, her sugar & spice
spent like grammar in a one-room

school house, an after-school bully
coming down hard, teach you
to suck up, a pet

to put down. Make a start
with this pelt. Much
to be worn. A catwalk

for China's air champ's
defining moment: at times of proliferation
the appellations are uncontrollable. If

you're not satisfied with the arrangement
that's implied by this less than compatible
orientation consider it a consequence

of dividing his rule. Let's tie
our legs together. Go horns
to the art party. Transition

from art to medicine. Did
it hurt? You bet. Made a mess
of his nest. Nurse

won't clean it. What
a tease! Mum's her word, his
too. How far

is God's house? Too far to walk
with that walker. Won't get
very far: Duffer escaped! Hot

on his trail. Catch & connect. Too
easy. What went wrong?
Lamp fright.

Vocalese

Dump & jive. Think you're wise just because
you roll. In point of fact you just a hate machine
on three wheels that got stood up on a ladder
five miles high. See this stackin'
it's not for you. Most couples hay make
nicely & with no needles but you, Miss Jones, you seem
so isolate on that bed going through the motions
of a one-night stand, hardly what
the mothers taught. As chuffed
as a tidal nothing on the cusp of something
grand, your cheer as graced as a cereal box
ring at that wedding where the groom
was shamed by Lady Lupin's timely query: "What's
the hush?" So quick to get your maids
of honour dressed thimble, broom
& shoe were little more
than a kitchen force, their nattering
of no avail. "We meant to curtsey
but couldn't bend." And Billy's
best man font? – clogged
with syrup, not punch
like our mothers made. Flip & fly, think
you're wise because you're droll, a talk machine
on three wheels, all flat.

Of Those Cut

Of those cut
we're especially fond. On them cast
sanctuary smiles that for sheer bounty
there's no beat to muster
the best of them. On that larnin' spree
the more the soldier us
who failed so miserably as did the Preacher
in the *Book of All* who failed to source
that Saxon mess. Had them on a chew
o yes he did, with a full plate
& a Salamanca shine as burst with life as seven
in a closet. Come out (wherever you are) it's
time for that couple feat that vestal you
so righteously shunned.
                    We will, but not until
everything's ripe & among the animals is
equally distributed that then for something better (more
appropriate) we might exchange that holy flesh that must
mean something for a gift name that obviously at
first reading does & will, called, render old noise, every
curse & mercy pleading, new.
                  So who, what fool,
you hurtin' on? Who slice for sport? Who fleece
for fun? Which voice in the hearing of this Fritz diminish
who does dread so well, will open veins for an audience
of two or even one? Mama move up & take
that razor away, no tear let make in some
not known. Let, Mama, no crazed cut
make wonder more.

The Burst the Vicksburg Bag Ensemble

As fail-safe as fax sex
you're clenched for a Catholic exit, Evangelists
knocking on your door. Which way
to milk culture? White

of you to offer a wolf hustle when, as
everyone knows, you've yet to grasp
the meek lamb technique. Methinks
you're something of a hypocrite. If only

what you listen you could speak through
Day-Glo teeth to a multitude packaged
for appeasement it could sooner than a spoon
stack a teacup storm for in-house gallants

who can't connect what modesty must best
or least. Believe in angels? Fairy tales
come true? Yes, but at Fedora
I cut off, a concession to Sam

who goes with gospel further. With him
it's a new soft us, a goodness shave
as close as feathering it in Memphis
I'll hold you true (I feel I must) to something,

to what? It might as well be Memphis, to Memphis
that you're held for it was there on a history boat
(O mighty Mississippi) that I met my mystic, my
hallelujah echoing from wolf to lamb

as the rending began
as the reading ended not
as you expected in face
of Law itself but with

as told the only thing he talked
what sat to his taste it recognised
to him a distant garden where so true
was how they said (as shrines break

cups & saucers) Me! Me! Me who
were ten without becoming, who had idols
more than one, who were
too many teeth that must chew

what's close & small. If appalled
consider it a calling, you the one & only
if clenched you stay, Evangelists
knocking on your door.

Cautionary Tales

Is this page scribble-ready?
Possibly, but how the word?
That match, I watched it sitting on my hands.
So sad how they stumbled, were trampled.

Meanwhile Putti pull aside the curtains & there:
the Poet presented to the people! Fifty plus
for that turpitude, fifty more if scant can clad!
Can you believe that harem's ripple?

If you're looking for Jesus you'd best start
with Jumper's Coke & listen carefully to Mutt's palaver.
If you want you can have my scare.
For size there's a pinch.

We could spend the day rowing.
I'd rather count pebbles, sort them as to color & shape.
My days of riding shotgun for nannies are over.
Who should we say *Hello* to? Who *Goodbye*?

Don't late please.
There's a huge lock on this forest.
We'll need at least an hour to pick it.
The gamekeeper arrives at eight. He's never late.

Sung out of wedlock: I'll go for that.
Prayed over by proper citizens, that too.
Of course I'd like to have a kingdom to call
my very own. What would you call it? *Rogue-on-Rye*.

Three guesses who left the chamber pot (full)
on the stove – Girl Guides to the rescue.
The apparatus of matriculation is too arduous
for my taste (haste makes waste).

Not only did Cinderella leave us her slipper
she left instructions of what not to do with it:
(1) don't ejaculate into it. (2) don't try to imagine
what it's like to *pussy-foot*.

Those dancing pimps how many were there, six
or seven? Seven. What's-his-name – Marat – that guy
who invented the bathtub, he forgot
to cross the *t* in tub.

Scribble ready? Yes, but how the word?
As to prayer, crawling? Curtains aside
by Putti? Pulpit-speak, a message for the people?
Come a cropper he'll be torn apart.

Pillow Talk

Struth, it's an evacuation. Go ahead
slap a scream on this face. It counts – how
you wear your slippers. How
did you just slip by? What ointment

judiciously applied? You must be
some mighty somebody. Let me hear it:
"I'm a mighty somebody!" Too bad
you're so thin. Nothing left

to yowl at soon. Welcome to
Joe's Place (a pickup bar), a perfect place to practice
your notorious servitude. Down on all fours,
what instinct will guide these girls

to a right & proper choice? "Luv me
luv my gadget. My only season
is a scold. I'm $100, not a cent more.
If I choose to sulk I will; you & your ilk

won't stop me." Mean in September, she's
meaner still in October. Pretty haughty
for a mama with carnival eyes. Statement
of intent: Embrace penury. There must be something

we could insinuate here. Some Johnny Valentine
flourish? – Too early to tell for sure but
we're thinking that maybe this baby's bacon.
"It make me scare, this baby talk." So late

in the day, too late to get naked. Who forgot
the chatter spouse? OK, big mouth, bring
your black-belted self on over here. Left to you
you'd stock a rainbow with flying fish. How dumb

is that image? Very. For sure it's not the one
that will make you smile. That comes later, in
the last paragraph, if at all. Meanwhile
I don't need yours I've got my own hair

comb ritual, a bit heavy-handed but
it's got me lookin' good, yes? Go ahead, just
this once, admit I'm the handsome one, you
the ugly. Try to get used to the fact

that you're a churl, one of those run-
of-the-mill folk who half a chance would beat
me silly for revenge. What I did wrong: Got tight
last night with Lil Pete Fuzz, super prophet, his

doom say if we don't, etc. Which the case – time
to quick-smart up Lack-o'-ham Highway straight
in Hell direction, fire-walking all the way. Struth,
a curse from a mouth, it's an evacuation.

Testicle & Tomb

A deaf ear to the slut that I am is a matter
of some urgency, scam doctor filching my tune
for a Mighty! So deserving, but all I get
is a one-off lay
                 too meager for a naked & paraded
self such as myself. Such chilly
undress, could a corset at least. Please,
less nag in sex style:
                 Provocations
put to rest. Done, but who shall daily cover me
who want only (before longer in tooth) to be
rigorously unpublished?
                 Amen. Alibi. Argue
that best wage is paid by Davy (Jones), a hulk
for the milks of war, wet nurse asking me how serve
my mental sites.
                 Easy, place me something to eat on table
of no risk, among knife & fork never boy again, no more
interrogation by bread & vegetables, abled
only to love hungry
                 (may illustrious remains constrain
my concern! – that nurse a lady in waiting?). She got
some nerve. In her soil am I drilled? So soon to sink
somewhere, goal via covert?
                 O Chichi AND
Chacha! O nothing in kiss felt! Have arrived
at end side only! No voice (me) since capture, my
chronicle cold as a cod.
                 This last clearly a case
of lunatic-speak squandering its not-so-chaste
deliquescence on an astrologically incorrect
no-fault prognosis,

the local abbey with its
rule of thumb (keep 'em dumb) not
taken into account, the kneeling nuns as one
turning to stare.
They know that tomorrow
at a café in Managua a madman will approach & throw
a tightly-packed ball of flowers at me, a mischief
toppling me.
Get up off that floor
'fore I exhibit! Look & learn. It's
a bum fight in Bombay. It's End Time
for Tea Party grunts.
They'd have me (me)
believe that of my birth to chance there is
no convenience, that, jaywalking, I'll get
a strawberry fine.
Where best
to die. Moscow? Kinshasa? Listen:
hooves in the kitchen: clip-clop, it's time to drop
pretence, my horde
of surgical instruments circa
1880 too rusty to use anyway, not even
on you. O would I had not seen what you wrote – *Love
handles on a charging rhino!*
So nothing for it but to skip
that scam doctor call, his insufferable prognostications, his
love-mongering probes, & turn a deaf ear to his nag, my
sex style not his concern.

Asylum Queries

Ask.
You won't receive but ask anyway.

Snagged on concubines, can you unsnag?
Comeuppance relinquished, who'll take the bow?
Your paper on the Residua of Transgression has yet
   to be tabled. How much longer must we wait?
These pills packed with the stuff of the exhumed. What
   are they good for?
Can't you see that we're too old to stoop to pick a peck
   of peppers.
We're getting a bit tired of kippers & mule meat.
   Any chance you could substitute peas for the kippers?
The sins of the cook's cat should not be conflated with ours.
   Why have they been?
Coffee percolating in Aunt Ruth's slightly-the-worse-for-
   wear vacuum cleaner. Do you really expect us to drink it?
Why must it be so heavy? – takes four of us to lift this
   wine-brimmed vessel to your thick, threat-sprouting (spill
   a drop & see what happens) lips.
Why is it a problem if we propose a toast to the Sioux, the
   treacle of tom-toms in our cups?
About the accommodation: why won't you concede that
   living in an elephant's carcass is not conducive
   to good health?
We know who the sane are & where they're hiding.
   They're hiding under your skirt. Why
   have you given them sanctuary?
Louise the Voluptuous, she loves to shimmy in a gossamer
   gown with lunatic fringe. Where's the harm in that?
Harold has a meter long penis, a source of
embarrassment,
   if not to him, to those who are not so
   magnificently endowed.
Those osculations you want us to experience, blindfolded,

tied to chairs, what effect will they have on our already
dubious equilibrium?

When are you going to have it fixed? – that smell we know
so well (burning flesh), the ECT machine always
overheating after the sixth zapped patient.

The tram that used to run through our ward, why have you
diverted it to the "dirty ward"?

Hair-thin, razor-sharp, the Sirat Bridge. Whose lamb,
sacrificed, will see us across?

Why must we always ask if we've checked our weapons
at the door – those knives, forks, spoons, napkins & the
occasional cup we've liberated from the cafeteria?

Why this fuss over a furphy? Surely you're not going to
flag us for an inveiglement?

For wool we languish. Why must you shear every day?

If your goal is to exfoliate our curls why did you censor
our lays with the bald?

When your scavengers finish with us why must they curtsy?

Equally scathing about Vet Bacon & Nam Style, where
would you have us file our complaints?

Why can't we keep the lollipops that Dolly doles out?

And that, esteemed sir, is just the tip of the iceberg.

Ballet Mécanique

As subcutaneous as picket-line plumage, ring-barked
spruikers spew peacock sludge on victim theory, all
in a night's work. Bastards, we cop it sweet
in the offshore sense of inept papacy in a room all doors

shredding relics, surveillance videos paused forever.
Bastards, they climbed my boat, took my bucket,
filled it with calf horns, cuckoldry livid with anti-
vivisectionist double talk. So what you mean by

honour song? Dosage nil? Reshuffled consolations
admonishing sales-pitch? As sad as the milk (sour)
of human kindness taking another hit we get the stunts
wrong, again/cut. At this rate there won't be a wrap

until the cows come home – a tracking shot
focused on... yes, you guessed right: milk, its process
(progress) as reliable as real estate coming clean
on the history of that gussied up whaling station, ours

for a song. *It must finally*
become serious (Marion). We've had our fill
of your tickertape nostalgia for in-harness road-kills, every
loving spouse out to conjure a perfect death for Jack

or Jill, joy ride thrills as cheap as cavalry
as the credits roll, any hijack much preferred to this
would-be wunderkind soundtrack with its squeals
& catalogues of woe, chuck-a-wobble English

drowned out by moratorium, more junk for Lady Jane's
Séance Museum, free entry, no exit. No excuse
for this post-coital grave stink you've been warned:
bathe in shuttle, in metaphysics, in remedial

pawnshop whatever it takes the denouement (in case
you haven't noticed) is already upon you, talk-back radio
settling your account with a cortege of closed-circuit icons,
you & your poppycock icons shuffling the light-fantastic.

from the Roadkill Variations

What am I getting at (what's being gotten at)? – the Fact:
Dead, or soon will be, told (man to man by Juan) how
my portrait will end – as a subject for the acolytes
of the Djibouti School of Psychoanalysis. For sure

they've got my number, & would have me hike
skirt which I'd gladly if I had one. Who
am I kidding? These acolytes are onto me. As one
they point to my closet even as every turn

of the carousel brings me closer to *happiness*. No,
I'm not going to get off. I've grown very fond
of this prancing horse. A proud pupil of Meister
the Bald, why would I not be? – his bevy

of Pony Girls mine to inherit if I can just hang in
for a few more hours. Yes, I admit it, it's obviously
my worst proud – profoundly fenced, flanked, hedged in
by some ink-fool's treasure shrugged off as trumpery. Try

aching with closure, a conjure with chaste & you'll know
what I mean, what it's like to be stuck in Sal's saddle as
fast & furious as that last goodbye: "Amigo, may
the Ten Sages of Leather make a bridle

of your insufferable prognostications" – those
self-serving lullabies without a hope in hell of extrapolating
Item Number 3532 from the Do-right Agenda, St. John
of Cod testing the libidinous effect of a pachydermatous

affront on steam punk camera buffs taking my picture
for some already-obsolete posterity – of me hung
in chains in Eden's dungeon, caught red-handed peeling
language from flypaper. Reach

for a star, get bitten. The bath? I'm just circling it
& will be for a month of roses, gladiatorial stink
not my thing. The plunge? To my shame
I can't take it until I've fixed the circus with a pin

as you would a butterfly & then (yes, I've been warned)
I must, I simply must stop prodding the shoemaker's kids
when they get on my nerves, not their fault that I'm three
sizes too small, my shoes that is. *One more Freudian*

slip & your day pass will be revoked & your tresses
sold to the highest bidder – two dollars & counting... Can
Sigmund or anyone for that matter calculate the irreparable
damage already done? Maybe, but don't

hold your breath. Don't show Sylvia your willy unless
you want your dosage upped three-fold, remedial drones
honing in, eye candy capitulating to voiced-over repeats
of the usual poppycock admonishments: skip the stun-gun

hustle & pour the wine, not transubstantiated but it's
good enough for what you've got to do – expose the
acolytes for what they are (wannabe Pony Girls)
& get rid of whatever it is that's being gotten at.

Zero Itinerary

Theft dressing not legit, too scrambled. Let
it rip? Better a gag order that makes no sense
to Al Aqsa's Mosquito Clan with its five year plan
but does to me: Time
to roll out those perennial favorites: Grandiose
Primping! Zero Itinerary, Jackboot Shame! Every story
a sob? The Heart Throb one (for example) that can't hack
Turkish Delight? Or the one about
those rent-a-mouth grammarians – *Let's tout*
while we can, stunt & slam soon upon us – yes, sad
& doubly so for what these snivellers are snivelling about
could be cured once & for all with a giggle, a gosh
what a wee willy, a catamite's slam. Dunk
those doughnuts, boys. Methinks
that what you want, what you really want
is that long-promised Punishment, & not just parcelled out
a chunk at a time, but all of it, the whole shebang,
now! *Give it to us hard!* – a sex change story
that gives the lie to that scam to maximize
humiliation when grammar goes, as it must, off
the rails for the nth time, indelicate maybe but
the confessions that follow from will gag Al Aqsa's
Mosquito Clan with its five year plan while we put paid
to Legal Tender's insinuation that we're all dressed up
(to the nines) with nowhere to go.

Follow the Money

Gimmie sass (cash).
Don't spoil.
Bible long time.
Every suck's a breeze.

He's a big well-read.
He's a must-see Tom.
Another ugly sky-scream.
High-speak off record (is official).

This business of dumb.
Give a man to talkin' (androgynous inceptions).
It's another *Grab some happy*.
We're live in Texas too.

Her gab stealing the show.
Kinfolk puckered for
Candy shop kiss.
To what must we sequence?

Sometimes people same people.
O to see that big jig shine!
To edit what we look like.
A pause for a yield.

That misconception got brother a bad reception.
No enticement in this position.
No sex with that mother/daughter combination.
In ten years maybe.

Sexy Spicy

Miss Gift, it's me, the one & only.
Who here can help crime?
In Detroit nobody dumb.
It's the town of Ray.

Look to Pity to keep relation.
You'll never know that side of face.
For how long you been on that gross feed?
For more important discussion push tab A.

Want to hear some high class?
Will they arrive in the nick, the CD/TVs?
Plays us best if we dress up?
You know it's not legal done.

Cotton pride my thing.
Can I strip you alive?
No sassafras in my past.
Meek or mean, whichever works.

Of course I'd like to see you make a show of weeping.
Your daddy is a tease
My girl so hot she shake three legs.
Let Speed come through clean.

Should this be a man's moan by women heard?
On this line (the 22nd) we must finish. Must now
tell true. Must readers inform how sick this circus is.
But how? Lion, horse, dog, clown all lost in some

New Age visualization technique I could never
get the hang of, too venerable (read vulnerable)
for mantra-mumble, kundalini peekaboo, pick
a peck of peppers, raven got your eye, etc.

Given

that the mad will bless us with befuddlement, all of us, each
    & every, on October 31st, 2024,
that this being the case who will protect my mother, dead
    these many years, from the machinations of the crib?

that Clive Palmer's Titanic will be torpedoed on my 87th
    birthday (January 10, 2024),
that this being the case it's obvious that the wolf will never
    lie down with to the lamb.

that these ham-fisted rednecks will have my guts for garters
    if I can't whistle Dixie to their satisfaction,
that this being the case it's obvious that the stench
    of the human will articulate the body's oink.

that the gosh & golly of Simon's impermeable perambulations
    will not be heard in time,
that this being the case it's obvious that the infidelities
    have become bloated past all reckoning.

that the child-bearing stork has not built its nest in our chimney
    & never will,
that this being the case it's obvious that Revelation has left us
    with a dozen eggs, all broken.

that the Gadsden Purchase can't be justified by the Gaia
    hypothesis,
that this being the case it's obvious that no livery, however holy,
    will deliver us from an audience where capitulation is a must.

that it's a fact that she's very much at home on this bed
    that she shares with the incumbent,
that this being the case it's obvious that the preamble
    was not the incontrovertible truth we thought it was.

that it happened in Granada where gallant audacity feeds
    whichever wherewithal feels the most astute,
that this being the case it's obvious that Miss Speed is not
    a proper royal.

that Pedro had the nonce to put it thus: "This death
    don't come cheap,"
that this being the case it's obvious that the last laugh
    we heard in Minneapolis found a home in Texas.

that there are consequences if you commandeer pedestrians
    for your passion play,
that this being the case it's obvious that Comrade Omar
    is here for the kill.

that I've had four near-death experiences, the last in India in
    1990 at the hands of 16 thugs with lathis & one with a hatchet,
that this being the case it's obvious that the chatter won't stop
    until the day of my death, January 10, 2037.

I See You

If you went to a Roman sale via Bach you'll know
what I mean when I say: *Trannie's girl suffered the most.*
That line you just wrote it's three years out of fashion.

You should have known not to take on a crawler,
let her squat in your happy home –
24 hour naked, DC crimp, not needful

for any song, yours included. I declare
I've never seen so much worse as this worse, what
I say: *Don't care if you suffered the most it's time*

to hit the road.
Miss Stealth Lee
I see you.

Friday November 11, 2016 (Black Friday)

Doors

I'm lying on a trolley, waiting.
In a pasture as green as the Green in Gables.
At the far edge are seven doors, closed, no walls, just
doors etched against a cloudless sky.
Come night, I'll be pushed through one of them.

Testing

I'm testing with my tongue: the taste of the paint on the
walls of this corridor; the noise in the rooms on either side;
the smell of the nurse who is speaking to me.
So far so good.
I can take a few more steps.

The Measure of a Man

What are they saying, the whisperers out in the corridor?
Something about 20 fingers long, 5 wide.
Lying here in my bed unable to sleep, am I 20 fingers long,
5 wide?
Of course it depends how long the fingers in question are.
Mine, apparently, are *average*.
So if the fingers in question are not average then the
whispering could be about someone else, about some other
patient in this hospital for incurable insomniacs.

Page

I've been here for three days. I've been waiting for someone
to come into this room & turn the page.

239

Pretty

Pretty doing as it pleases
does me no favours. Seven years
for that miserable Phoenix to rise, I'll never pass
for a Rosen(berg), thugs at my door
just in case. And in any case I buried
that clunky typewriter in Pete's Bog two weeks ago,
good riddance! – an end to that questing vexed
by a swank, tooled by a taunt. "Betcha
can't mount this penny farthing & pedal thyself
elsewhere, away from here." "If Payback
doesn't absent you I will!" – Fast-tracked
to sapphics, slogans, muzzlements, drones, a glib
ministry to a klatch of child brides. So pretty! Anyway
here I am all over the *word* – pummelling & patching &
God knows what else. If you've been as *spoken for game*
as I have your deportment – crawling – would be
as suss as mine. What I mean is: languishing in latex
you could be mistaken for the creaking of a ghost ship's
rotting timber. "It's hot in here; I don't want to play
any more." Spoiled me, as Pain backs me away
from Pleasure I'm reminded of that old saw: don't
swim if you can sink, the provenance of which
is a basket with a babe abandoned in a heaven-
tusking forest of spruce & mandible
where evidence is tainted by chronicle: who had
& who had not (show me your fat I'll show you
my lean).
There, it's off my chest; I'm clean.

A Nuptial

Hanging out in Hamburger Hell
who ordered the butterscotch sandwich? What
the dying do is twitch. Pony Brag
is a right bitch. Him astray,
it's a microphone joke. Giving himself food he stood
to watch his plate, that it would not empty. Where
are we anyway? – American Combat
stuck in mud. Dig in. Stay put. Don't acknowledge
the subprime punks at the next table, that huff & puff,
those tails that wag. Willy so wee, can't get no… And Jim
(Jim Dandy) who did us proud at that max absorption gig;
too bad he blew the ethical nutrients quiz. It's not
your average Joe Blow with his born-again delectations
that's got Widow Brown's dander up like a cut-loose kite,
little Henry home in tears, it's being told that where
we stand is not a standing place. G-up & fly then? Or prove
that scar? Who on thee lavished? And (confess) did it wash
with our lady of whom you speak so bountifully? Your
bouncing baby boy, Mother, I'm threadbare. I want
to know what keeps me from my nifties – the Nines, they
do, for they beget a bold Brazil. And the Fives, for they
a saucy French. Now that
is bad. It's an inarticulate I'll have none of. And worse,
crossing Broadway against the light: a dozen giant crows
with human feet. Please, this silly hallucination dispatch
quick. If ever cream (the vanishing kind) was needed it's
now. Pony Brag, you could at a gallop bring. Or with
a wallop scatter the spooks, eyes on me, it's just not right.
From view lost, finally? Not a chance. Hey, there's

me old mate, Miguel. What's he doing with that blue
rooster – holding it up for all to see, bloody spurs, crowing:
VICTORY! Last seen, Miguel, at that dancehall in Mombasa, The
Three New Eden, cheek to cheek with Kesi
& Kibibi & off to the side, waiting, the predators – jackals
& hyenas; they came by dhow; satiated, they'll leave
by dhow, red sails, dawn breaking. Miguel: *if we can do*
the broom with Kesi & Kibibi we can do anything, right?
I'd certainly like to think so but… well, we seem to be
caught up in American Combat, stuck in that mud &, no,
it wasn't me; I didn't order this butterscotch sandwich.

Safari

Sixty tigers dead & we've only just started.
If you mess with Mabel we'll surely crash (she's driving,
in case you haven't noticed). Don't ever mistake
the M-4 for the I-66 again. Yes, that's a threat.

Tumbled from Lot's bed, they made us kneel for prayer.
That echolalia (plus helicopter gusts) has the stretcher-
bearers confused – who to carry first & where? And more
to the point – are we listed? – lunatic, looney, headcase,

nutter? In short, in *The Natural History of Insanity* Fritz
Waugh got it wrong. The loss of that shoe had nothing to do
with that failed coup. So back to basics: this *Who's Who*
has the Comeback Kid in bed with Louise when in fact

she's not his squeeze & never was. If we drink to that
will the Kid be offended, pull out a gun, bang? – A coffin
on wheels pulled by a snow-white mule, now that's
what I call style: when we race, me & brother, in the scald

car we race Nam Style & beat File Bacon. Beat by a mile,
so why you ask us speak Mama when everybody know
she the same side we carry sister? Can't answer that
can you? Is why we've got a photo of you nailed

to the mast: wanted, preferably dead. Staggering up
the toy-strewn gangway, drunk again & there you go,
down like a beer keg; bad luck/good riddance/anchors
aweigh. What a sorry town – abandoned brothels, empty

theatres, a rotting manta ray on the Town Hall steps, drops
of blood from the beak of a fighting cock leading us…
nowhere. Why did we follow them? Hoping for what?
That wall-eyed whistle blowers will wash up

on Muscle Beach & win the under fours sack race?
God help us if they do we'll need at least a week
to recover if we're lucky, haven't worked out yet how
to avoid those rent-a-crowd angels who, half a chance,

will slap us at breakfast AND lunch AND dinner: smack
smack smack & no dab (just a little would do us), would
send those chattering penitents on their merry way
down Yahweh Lane. God speed, & may your tinkering

with clapped-out demarcations prove beneficial to
those Bible louts under the care of Father Brown riding
rough through Roosevelt, Pocatello off to the left. What's
left is nun-tease & a smidgin of hagiolatry with a soft spot

for scam talents. Which is where we come in/back
for an encore – same old razz but, hey, listen to this
new matazz: we're armed to the teeth & out for game,
sixty tigers dead & we've only just started.

Hermeneutic

Whatever it is that Similitude puts up & decides
I've had enough of – that slippage
from the oud player's oval mouth to
these two prophets battling it out on a raft
with vision sticks: "Whatever else it might be
it's against death, this poetry!" Not
to be dead again. Fat chance. Count to 3 – that shuffle
to the left, then to the right. "Is this what the pill does?"
No choice, I'll go, why not, with the game: pitter-
pat, doctrine-snap. Careful, Doc's about to make
a Gilles de Rais gesture, takes out scissors, cuts (one snip)
my hair; takes out an alphabet, stuffs it into my mouth.
"Chew on that, asehole." A lot to swallow, A to Z, Braille
that the blind insist on touching (it tickles) in the corridor
that serves as my throat, inevitable collisions "Watch
where you're going." Cane fights. You think
it's a joke –Ha Ha – when it comes to throes
you're a stumblebum, a hopeless novice. So what
can you do to liven up this poem if that's what it is
that you've already had more than enough of? Introduce
convulsions? – convulsionaries in wheelchairs doing
what they do best: convulsing. Now wasn't that
exciting. And for an encore: sharks swimming
in the foyer of this fleabag hotel. Death by shark bite:
another issue on which I'm soft, although
when it comes to the guy next door with his radio tuned
24/7 to the *races* my rage is palpable. So what
am I lacking? I'm lacking a loon (as in tune), "Chew
on that, asehole." And know that this ah shucks

collaboration between Able Now & Ben Bush is only
45% & that this high-octane go-get vociferation will NOT,
repeat, will NOT have a happy ending because, despite
appearances, I'm not one of your heartthrob arrivistes
strumming on an oud. "Is that what the pill does?"

Love Song in B Flat

It was a sickness day.
Mad that way & the better for it.
Moro had no obligation to.
His slide was gravel-fraught
with frowns on either side.
You can do it!
Three parts neurosurgeon, one part nurse.

Moro back to buy a frock a saltimbanque was there
with a smock nail. It was a way to let the birds. Of looking
air & cloud. Of sycophants, that when they launch
a watcher that upon you spying
you'll need to buy one too, a frock.
You can do it!
Three parts tranny, one nurse.

A narrow plank over a pit: the lost
in a crouch, an axolotl crouch. Why always
that what I know is increased by balance failure? Even
though I don't do topple it's nevertheless done –
a plunge, a membrane tumbled through with grace.
You can do it!
Three parts funambulist, one nurse.

How mummy & daddy got dirty,
now there's a story: Radio Baghdad
buck-tinged, calling for yokels – caught
in the Caliph's kitchen, to whom to run?
Not to dirty mummy, not to dirty daddy.
You can do it!
Three parts eunuch, one nurse.

Are you pupillary invested?
In oracular is how you put you for to write?
By which time plenty congress.
By which is meant to follow the aficionado tongue
to organs, skin, muscles, etc.
You can do it!
Three parts scribe, one nurse.

How prepare a popinjay for cohort ?
Did you at least think Perdition?
Too late to dad's trap mechanism – empty.
Could better have said how reason schemes hide.
No more discussion of crazy please.
You can do it!
Three parts oracle, one nurse.

Mother rang, she wants a toggle
for that Christmas switch. If
I'm going to hitch my life to yours
I want some compensation, your collection
of Ethiopian stamps for a start.
You can do it!
Three parts bride, one nurse.

Multiplicities unleashed, the epics
are poly, are numerous
with Adorno-speak. Looking Krakow,
is that still possible? Mort meanwhile
is standing still; he has no boogaloo to do.
You can do it!
Three parts dead man, one nurse.

Kitchen Fame

Where else would I be cookin' if not in the kitchen?
Those boy rags, they won't tear. The way Deb
dresses down, it suggests that Pennsylvania lives
don't matter. Risk mother, she'll leave us

with something less than precious. No truck
with a union force, that's my motto. Is naked
always true? After you've made your peace
with the po-lice you can dial & leave. When Thurber

says *Hark!* he means it. No matter what we urge
it comes up short. No more big man
on the tambourine. Smart guy, you'll shipwreck
that history boat; you'll crash that vanity car. Homing

through fog, no one will hear those shop-worn
moans. That horn has Mother orbiting. Who, if
not you, should she give that talking to? Rendered
intelligible, you're unshackled. You do flap-flap, fife

& drum leading the way. Step carefully, elude
the signs. They're everywhere. For example:
these Pythian teeth. Hail them not & likewise
Apollo's penis. That fool

would have you kneeling. You wanna
make conceit? Go ahead, no skin
off these knees. If it's ad hoc
it's not negotiable. Down Bella Road in that fat

Cadillac what in Christ's name are we coming to? – Wall!
Wire! Dogs! Over there, other side (wall scaled) it's Sick
Nation Week. Take issue with? I most certainly will with
a great blooming booming baptism, soak your sorry ass

to the marrow. You'll wish you had gills. Hurry up,
peel off, full immersion for the likes of you. What wouldn't
I do to put to rights this water baby's pride? I'd never bring
a Rasta home, dreadlocks played for a stash. Beats me

why everyone want a little somethin' to tide over with.
If you really must over Thurber enthuse please do.
I'll never blame. To quote David wa Maahlamela re Robert
Mugabe when I pray for forgiveness I'll mention your name.

Saints' Days

Paul the Hermit January 15 Arising from Sleep: let's
collude in something I don't care what so long as in
your ass-grabbing enthusiasm you don't rub that
death-infatuated genie's lamp.

Polycarp February 23 Grace Before & After Meals: slip
into something a bit more comfortable, something
a bit more as it were marinated that what we'll sup on
tonight won't be the usual unpalatable mess.

Cyril of Jerusalem March 18 Stations of the Cross: this
scene & the thirteen that follow are much too photogenic
for the likes of you. Cut them all.

Francis of Paola April 2 Acceptance of Death: in
the precinct of moles cybersnaps account for the summer
& fall extinctions. One can only surmise that those tucked
away in burrows are waiting for some winter ritual.

Celestine May 19 For the Sick: as for compassion save it
for that dowager in doldrums because I won't wear
her soiled panties to my coming out ball.

Emily of Vialar June 17 For Employment: tender
enough rope to sufficiently bind her – wrists, thighs, ankles –
for a proper suspension, arranging Madam's whips
by sting the task to which I've been assigned.

Bonaventure July 15 Act of Contrition: through the Souk
of Humility I'm piggybacking Mother on the condition that
through the Souk of Ham she'll piggyback me.

Sabina August 29 For Charity: tonight, in alignment with
a certain star (that won't be named), I'll couch alone, a ham-
fisted masseuse marvelling at the wastage of my thighs.

Salvius of Albi September 10 In Time of Anger: let
these cane-wielding fugitives prod us wherever they feel
they must for tomorrow, these birds of a feather
in gilded cages, it's our turn.

Frumentius October 27 For Purity: who lost the key
to the cabinet where we've hung enough rain to feed, drop
by drop, the candles that keep the snow-white bodies
of our children warm?

Castorius November 8 Take me from the dark: why ask
what use an axe if not to chop when I know the answer off
by heart (& in the right order) – ankle, rib, finger, forehead.

Olympias December 17 The Seven Sorrows: a wake
I should be in awe of – my Seven Vanities banging like
cans behind a honeymooners' car, but I'm not; they mock
me every night, those little deaths that rattle in my throat.

Forensic Delights

A wink & a nod usually enough to secrete them away
for a month or two – the polyglot kissers, the
surrogate wives. Learn to love my bright bites, my winks
& licks & kicks or do without I couldn't care less

that I care even less for these lockdown nerds who wheel
Mother in for a feed – bacon on cheese (Swiss). That hiss
got them guessing – lame geese in a bowling alley?
pumped men choking on pumpernickel? It didn't pan out,

that blind date with Mickey Rooney. Ali Baba
would have been a better choice. How soon
will she be ready? – that mare all painted up
with zebra stripes. By High Noon I hope

so's I can ride her into town, hitch her up in front
of Pete's Saloon, saunter in, guns blazing. Bad luck,
mom's got the drop on you. So much bother over a life
that given Grace by the bucketful is nothing more

than a purveyor of croons, luscious improprieties
to pleasure some fool who boarded a tram that simply
vanished as if poured into a cup & that cup drained
by a milk-toothed phrenologist who rants

for hours about the indignity of an uncontrollable
pirouette, my spin a sermon to a congregation
in pews on a beach, the Zeppelin overhead
about to burst into flame. What the Lord giveth

the Lord shall take away. My authentic Sioux moccasins
for a start & the patronage of Lady McGirth. Penniless
in Bedlam, my bob for a sanity apple comes up missing
myself, my glow in a blowhole, my pimp's roll

in undertow, Samatha yours for a pinch me sane
& Lucy the same. Zelda, now that's a different
kettle of fish: pay as you row, the kids in tow
dragging your shoes off & then your socks & the garters

that keep them aloft (why do they always keep
their shoes & socks on, the flappers & sailors
in those roaring twenties porn photos?). Why convulse
in 8/5 when you know you should in 4/4? Why infest

with shame my mayhem moments? Why question
the business-as-usual progress of my thrice-dead
mother's mother? For thrice is nice, it truly is its
neuronal liquidity a perfectly safe solution to

those data accumulations that all too often clog up
the end-time drip-feeds on Ward 6. Sex
at a premium: this vessel leaks, will not accommodate
a leg-up no matter how delicate the lift. Try it

& I'll blab it all over the town & obviously won't
omit the part where you're impounded for cruising
those habitats where marriage on the rocks scrolls
down to the lair of that bleeding-heart fascist

in mufti who insists that you type in *dog collar*
& watch what happens: men marching as to a war
that if you ask nicely you can embed in, in tight
with the polyglot kissers, the surrogate wives.

A Darktown Strut

Under the sign GLAD it's starting to hurt.
Soothe you with a Jersey stroll.
I wish I was a better me.
When you see that fool give him a smack.

Tell him it's from me.
To invent you properly I need six blue dogs
& a polka-dot sponge. Only five? Bring me that dog
quick or I spank, hard. What he said:

if Glory's a bee in a bonnet
Holy's a kick in the nuts.
Would you like to forage with me?
What you expect you come to this business

with a grin like that? What for
you choose that mongrel kitchen for a love-in? –
in high-heel crocodile shoes to parade among pots.
Look out, I'm about to shrink to a grown man!

That trick play me hell all night.
Gonna get me one of them offshore women.
Crooning's how I'll do it.
Little Roo came to my party.

She didn't stay long.
The gestalt: aberration in a charm region.
Who said Avarice has a pink lining?
It's brown. Silly me, I should have known.

There's a vamp in that camp.
No tent is safe.
Keep the tribe door shut.
Sorry about that backstab.

That three bead church got power.
And what I got was ten of Eve.
Why is it always *Used to be*?
Mother, I've much to shame.

How I like it? – Bold, bald & bad.
But please to tell: where the body that me can be?
If not in a mouth in what to believe?
What we need is a hoodoo (who dunnit) witness.

At Whisker's (Bar & Grill) I made a wish:
that a friend to Fury I'd never be.
She got on that phone & shivered.
I thought I told you to shush that motor.

Go ahead, show us your thirst.
Your hurricane ways aren't welcome here.
From coat to bull is a distance of one horn.
Bad at the door, you're worse on the floor.

Summer dazzle dumps Joan.
I may have blown my druthers but I know my potions.
Hog-tied on Cobbler's Hill, Jack's here but where's Jill?
Did Dub Ray do this?

Me & Gil, we missed out on the *We-care* caper.
I'm studying Old Jim's stutter-shuffle.
Might go that way myself.
Spurs dug in, she ride me night & day.

Humdingers

Whom they had broken a face
on the carpet formalities
where the second wrestling accrued
house patience was needed.

But none to spare, already by
all possible means the discussion
of Cicero opened the way
for a dalliance.

Best risk a polka
for a masculine spill so slow
is Mother teaching
The Felicities.

What took my notion
by surprise: that day creative
with cross-dress gossip, suit
& hair denied.

Covering & cowering
what is hidden tenders
what is never audible
to noise pretenders.

Who chew morning & night
refuse to endorse
the lost science
of correct positions.

Small uncleanlinesses
add mentality garments
to the contours
of ambiguity.

Future Pandoras
now strike
stinking
undesirables.

At the time of Beersheba
button men assumed
that the golly-golly
would last forever.

For longevity my hankering
is interrogated for possible
slippage, insufficient inoculation
the reason given.

Such was the luxury
in which he was embedded
that speckled barbarians
crawled in with him.

Lilting fictions
having had their day
'tis time for Zanele
to have hers.

Provisions for
clochard impregnation
at masked balls
are paramount.

Inviolable
the cascaras,
adorable
the mamalias.

Mother Chaos
fosters confusion
among the eaters
of verbiage.

She sickened
from too much wanton,
he because
he could not prey.

Served on a silver tray
the little delicacies
have swollen
with pride.

Ordinary suicide asking lace
to keep its treasure name
overlooks interventions
by the already volatized

Parricide
as an exercise in parsimony
forbids the gestation
of disdain.

Rococo

for Colin Rhodes

Pausanius, what's he got that I don't?
Dead crows in a hessian bag, three more
    than I'll ever have.
Some fool left his feet for us to fight over.
Chain me to that bed again
    I'll kill you once. I'll kill you twice.
    I'll kill you 24/7.
Injured in an owl fight, he died within the hour.
Eating raw chicken, bones & all, Echemus
    left nothing for the cat.
If no one objects I'll make that cat scat.
Did that scat go pitter-pat?
The reign of money's prerogatives in the respectable press
    is not compatible with the shrinkage of the man
    he'll turn out (after all is said & done) to be.
Left to himself in a corner he felt (at last)
    what made him good.
That holy concoction gave Aischylos diarrhoea.
Am I right? – it *is* the stuff of body.
Cancelled at mouth, that carry-on about which mob
    was the least likely to sympathise with your shenanigans
    was soon forgotten.
You got some nerve: detox on my watch.
Refusing to cook Mom's gruel, let go thy pride & serve.
If you burn down Dad's house (the white one on the hill)
    you'll be sorry.
Comic interlude: while we go for a piss
    Judy wallops Punch.

System Pop

The boy with a star splashed on his face
is clutching a serpent, symbol
of something, I don't know what. And
I don't know why or where they're going
if anywhere, these thirty floating corpses
(human) in the sky, not sky-blue, no, it's
marine green & down there somewhere:
tubas harrumphing, a symphony by Neptune. In this
& in the next (movement) the ocean is hidden
which of course implies that the creatures
immersed in it are hidden too. So where does that leave
the floating corpses (human)? I don't know. What
I do know is that when I come to your house
for dinner tonight it won't be ready, as usual. And so,
as always, I'll have to cook it myself. If only you knew
what's good for you you'd keep those blackbirds
in that pie, not let them fly around in the kitchen
shitting everywhere, making nests in our hair. In
a tattooed spiral around your left arm, shoulder to wrist
is the alphabet. On your right, shoulder to wrist, writ
small, the Gettysburg Address. So how about a bit
of emancipation for the kitchen slaves? This
was supposed to be a sonnet, but as it's already nine lines
too long will anyone object if we continue with an epiphany
of some sort? – Stabbed with a miniature Eiffel the hissing
cobra on the stove slowly expires. We might as well
have it for dinner. System pop.

Selfie

I tried the boats. They didn't work.
If I don't chase I won't catch.
One of seven I made my way to supper.
Beside my plate: six would-be eaters.
I came because I required to laugh stronger.
My harm is worth a pity, surely.
Yes, I rent your house.
I shine your shoe: shoe-fly-shoe.
You want to own what I own? Why?
Insect interrogation, am I that small?
Do them before they grow abundant.
Don't nobody move: my teeth is bein' picked.
Did I pause in the right place?
Split my britches, & more besides.
Cross my heart hope not to shame too much.
Pray for more preserve is my resolve.
If you think J. Finch is my man you're wrong.
Ran down Skeeter Jones, took what he had
Got all aimed up, & missed.
Is that the best banger you got?
I know how to bugle, & trumpet too.
Cup jumpin'/bottle waggin' I can do both.
That slippery-hand woman up & left me no moolah.
That temperature you talk is my face.
Turn that *What'd you say* off 'fore I break it.
I tried, I really did: to do some do-right in that do-wrong.
Down on 31ˢᵗ Street is where I tried to quit.
I tried a coat to bed.
As I did not think it necessary I did not try a hat.
Thank you for your satisfaction.

When All of Asia Sings

When all of Asia sings
woman peak at so & so, widows in mufti wandering
between obscene piles, the pro & con
of my obsession with toddlers with
suicide vests. As any service of a fundamental nature
excites a morbid curiosity among those who would show
the wolf to the door we'd like to know if, bottoms
up, the whole lot could be spanked in one go. And No,
they won't get off on the milk clause. It's obvious
that these babes are off their feed, milk flowing
in Paradise but not here. So please be informed
that the mix in this tale of woe is all wrong.
Straight ahead is Tallahassee (not Paradise)
& à gauche it's Paris where Francis (Picabia)
is cooling his heels at the Closerie des Lilas, no victory
for the spankers today. Estimable Sir, might I remind you
of that trip we took to Barcelona in your Bugatti, screaming
around curves on the Costa Brava, how tumultuous
that was. Loud & clear that roar of abundance! Fetch me
a star bag! Let dreadlock spoofs prevail while I stroke
a collared slave! And that Halie Selassie impersonation
what a grand idea! So let us not be concerned with
the noodling of Bunny Berrigan's trumpet wrath, tincture
superseding fracture by a factor of ten, this jaunt
with the signatories leaving us culpable? No, in
the big picture we're working the tables
at Breugel's, hustlers constructing for your pleasure
a jubilation, a juncture, a jinx (you know the drill): when
Jill shames Jack there's always a rugged-up Dutch
pointing the way to bread, pumpernickel not rye. Bye
the bye, of the many falsifications (in this poem) the
reference to the *love nest* (see line three) comes
within a smidgeon of some truth: that our sickness
is of a piece with that old saw – the mother of my friend
(Picabia in this case) is the mother of me – such minions
as we are of some pumped-up avant garde we do concede
that clock is best, river a gamble.

Stage Whispers

So perfect the permutations of the unflappable Mr.
George Ness-Elliot's ouevre that… Let
me get this straight, you take a darling give
her heart is a time-hounoured method of dealing
with that sense of foreboding when surrounded
by stage whispers left, right & center? Maybe, but
with the neighbourhood dogs barking 24/7 at one
or several of the local ghosts you'd do better
(at quelling that fear) if you sold sex
in a pup tent. Note: the fool in this poem
is Willem von Brasch. Would it please you
if I added a *von* to my name? If, a von, I accepted
my status as *chattel*? Worth how much
at the local slave market? Who be that, the ugly one
the punters ask. Surely not the guy who does
the Savornella impersonation at the Follies B. –
those bonfires of the vanities, that trial by fire gone wrong
they hung the bastard. Not likely, this guy's a voluptuary,
a would-be decadent in the style of the Parisian Hashishans,
Gautier & that lot. Which school
should I send my mother to? Pickaninny High
or Ibu Grammar? Not much difference, in both
they zero in on pork morphology, every table
in the cafeteria doubling as a hog market, buy one
get one free. Ha ha, you're about as funny as
a scolding wife in a barber shop. Short back & sides,
I went home with gold in my teeth. OK, so I'm willing
(& able) to use a shank. Does that make me
a has-been or a newbie on the block? That frock
you're wearing, isn't it the one that the Sundance Kid
was caught dead in? In for a tenner my gourmet instinct
pits Mother Porridge against Father Toast, guess
who wins? All along it was Bigger Tom who played
the sucker card, dad dumbed-down, outsourced
to Bacon Farm. In Harm's way, no coin (of any realm)
will buy me out & that darling, well, forget about her
she'll love it when I succumb to stage whispers, left
right & center.

Channeling

Now that we've kidnapped the Chinese
ping-pong champion (and taken his paddle)
please sit (there's an empty chair in this poem),
take a load off your feet & wipe that
I've *just been milked smile* off your face.
A little scholar telling his beads is all you are.
Might I suggest that you simply pop-off
à la mode & make some strickly local gesture
that makes of a politic a tusking service
for the dandies of this world, those lost souls
who brought us the yurt as a Quo Vadis lookalike, i.e.,
preach street smarts/come back to bite you
you know where. Surely you'd prefer
that I play you a music? – the conversation, for
example, of dead trees, or the crackle & snap
of love noise, limbs akimbo in frangipani, Lenny
masturbating behind a bush? Meanwhile
we got this guy tied to a chair in the cellar, what
to do? As stated by Rule 57 in the Book of Games
for Old Girls: when one encounters one of those trollops
of yesteryear run your fingers through her hair
while you intone the history of the glorious wars
she missed. In other words, how we pass the time
with Trish is none of your goddamned business.
Catch you cooking my goose, mister, King Ing
will have your guts for garters. Is mummy
still alive? Look, is that a legend
I just saw pass? How manifest? Has she sharps
on her person? Would us cut? Our melody
a malady? Undone by the onslaught
of a pan-pipes-in-the-background love interest
we acknowledge that in the end it's that dreaded
Minister for Sports who spoils our game & brings the poem
to a foregone conclusion: that, milked, we tried
but failed to channel the mutterings
of a Chinese ping-pong champion.

265

Pascal

Brag finished, Pascal repairs to bitch lair, puts
pen to paper: "Me no marriage chump
& furthermore I keep my person neat – which to say
that a dance at the Ball Bollier with some
Belle Epoque belle would probably tend
to set me up/put me in the running for
the status of *essential monument*, the mouths
of a dozen intriguers demeaning me: curly
& cheap & not at all of-a-piece (as he claims) &
not even remotely commensurate with any code
(of conduct) & with a paucity of amendment that defies
the servo gals who pump his gas. In short: should
be scuttled." To which: "To wit, brothers, I'm punctual
in Madrid & keep eating quietly when back & forth
waiters josh & immune to carte blanche I'll swap
your fo for your fum & of course I'm prepared to treat
Pugnacious Travel to a spliff &, yes, I'm pleased
with haberdash & if raincoats settle scud
I won't object." Brag done, Pascal back
to bitch lair: "On second thought
I might have been a marriage chump."

Of Maids & Milk

Don't come the runt with me.
I'll get riled up, spit a dummy, choke
on a word to the wise. Smart guy
I know you, you're that fool who reckons
that the whole world is just one big milk farm. Harm's
Way, I'm in it, in the path of, a she with a grimace
bedevilling me with spiteful enumeration: rake, roué,
debaucher, lecher, libertine... In short
oversexed & over here. Back
where I came from! – which farm won't have me, my
milking days too long over, a has-been dairy-maid, fingers
knotted with arthritis, joints too stiff for milk stool
articulation, ancestral limbs effervescing in back country
beds (matrimonial) that double as comfort stations
for the weary who have given up on those ladders
(out there in the paddock) that lean against nothing.
Go ahead, climb one, see where it gets you. When hook
& ladder men kiss we know it's time to celebrate (again,
how boring) the death by fire of H.K. Grossmann whose
only claim to fame was that he loved a lass back
in the day when one could play at scratch a back
or shame a goose & not be held to account. Allowing for
the manipulations of a Miss B. Witherspoon, hell
bent for leather pride slut, let's see what's left
of that mess – a black market (in milk)
turning white? The anniversary of a death
that hasn't happened yet, maybe tomorrow? Hang on,
let's wait for a weather forecast before we decide;
I don't know about you but I'd like to die on a hot
summer day, everyone in the procession throwing off
their clothes, a graveside orgy as the coffin is lowered,
that dummy spat.

Seraglio

Knocking on my door: Fatima & her sister Fatima.
If they can't stiffen my resolve nothing can.
Is there someone/anyone out there who can verify
the life of me? "If you're
that special someone who works behind a door
give me a call." Menacing wives
was my main game, probably
a bad choice. O harem, what batch
of stuff? What dream fulfilled carried of in a quick car,
hot mama at the wheel! Let me introduce myself: Willy
Quickstep by name, a wanton by trade. What
the mens say: *A felt stranger, watch me walk me.* On
my mind: everything that was once mighty plus
what to buy mom for Mother's Day. At bay
the Hicksville Hounds, Snap, Crackle & Pop. Cop
that, & that, & that! Teach you how to bubble & squeak
properly, no more poor me, Little Orphan Fanny
begging for nickels on mean streets. All
that I've heard, that's all I want. If it's not
too much trouble please take the trouble to show.
And make polite or: Impunity gets a slap! Am
I happy? You can bet your sweet ass I'm happy. Also
lucky & going to a spa to leave a smear It's
my campaign to eradicate that culture of a one-night
stand that's plagued me for years, that question
finally answered: When is a doll not a doll? For which,
the answer, a price to pay? – $10.52. Highway
robbery. Fifty-two cents too much. So as not to be
scammed by Widow Aisha & her fancy man, Ahmed
the Tooth, again my modus operandi from now on will be
the *violon d'Ingres,* i.e., debauchery in a seraglio.
If that's intolerable, as I'm sure it will be (for such
is the life of me) stop knocking on my door.

Big Shake

It's obvious; it's written all over your face.
You've been in the Land of the Immaculate Mothers
(again) & that makes you what? – a BIG SHAKE
(a BIG SHAKE with how many squandered love interests?)
for which: an appropriate punishment: You: trumpet stuff
with an unscratchable itch that can be likened to (dumb
simile) an often touted (tooted) mandrake root strangled
by ectoplasm (No, there won't be any more séances, no
more imperatives "to stylize one's body" for the gullible).

So, OK, the plot has thickened; we can live with that, our
Ritalin dependency a blessing in disguise. Also: Pork
Crime: Yes, we eat pig. And, Yes, we're well aware
that it's time to *slough off* (when the ball comes to an end
we'll disappear in a puff of smoke). Promise? You bet

& we'll take that mother-to-be, Marie what's-her-name, with us.
O happy scandal, look: it's Venus weeping over the corpse
of Adonis (who sloughed off big time). Time
to throw away our goblets & drink from our cupped hands.
Skoll! Salute! Bottoms up, etc.

"At eighty the tomb grows larger, the world smaller."
Who said that? It was said (as if you didn't know)
by the guy in the Ron Poster leisure suit, Prince Horace
Blackwell III no less as he stepped down
from a two-horse cabriolet, paparazzi flashing

that proverbial ectoplasm (No, there won't be…),
& made his way (minders punching paparazzi)
into the foyer of The Pyramid for a rendezvous
with (you guessed it) the Immaculate Mothers.

Tidings

Debauchers to the right, debauchers
to the left &.. (where's the justice?) our cantor, Peter,
sacked. Why? Simply because he refused
to censor. Consequently & therefore it's up to us
to purge the pink bits & fall to the Good, a country mile, the
Ancient of Days with needle & thread to mend & just
to be sure – a sloppy kiss. Wish you
a speedy recovery: in flagranti delecti
you'd best not be caught again. Reduced
to monoglot your fate if… And (also) vexed you'll be
by clerics, a routine they've got down pat. So no out, get that
into your head &, No, there won't be any pardon begging,
no crawl, no bow & scrape. And meanwhile our cantor,
Peter, sacked, time on his hands, indulges in a galumphing
jeremiad of on-a-stage strut He reckons the world is his
& all under, on & above it as well. Not quite
the case, for look, yonder, on high, in clouds, at
four corners, blowing, those cherubs repudiate
his latest – *Rococo* – ill conceived, as all, most, every
book of his is, excess not sweet, those horns
obstreperous, brash, rash & to no point the words
in it, this spilling-over tome with its obsequious
tidings all bad. But, look closely, in some, hidden
in plain sight, for your delectation, some pink bits.

Apocatastasis

Give me, Jesus, a break. Not another
intrusive voice, ten thousand too many
this week & it's only Monday:
"BY MOTHER CULLED": every tourist in town
in my bed, demanding service, six my limit.
                                        "You want
your house (only yesterday *put*) to stay in order PUT
OUT, be the defective you always wanted to be, i.e., embed
with the stanchioned, a salaam if you please
while they nurse their wounds."
                              What time
did time start for you? At 12:15, suss missionaries
schlepping for Mary who weighs what
a river weighs, tooth-wide, tongue-deep, Bo Peep
calling us home.
                  As we go we'd best
make it up, how in cribs they kept us green
& the gosh thereof was a bucket to bear
but no one could,
                    too cowed by a big girl story
we bowed to a purblind victory, a pummel
& purse. Which ruin was uppermost
in Danny's Bar & Grill,
                        Danny's theory of suppose
our couplings were in the grand style, on
his knee therefore placed for congress
correction,
            so vexed by quotidian parsing that
the much sought, finally found Apparatus would,
as foretold, fail, Benevolence Itself impotent
in the face of such.
                    Also, interlocutors voluble
with relics – why these conceal you on your
abominable person? To protect, good sirs, from
unwanted cajoling by seedy indigenes who late
arrive in swaddling clothes,

271

                             their purpose to mock
my liver-spotted nakedness in all corners come
what may, usually a bearing down by some vixen-
purposed enticement:
                             rice paddy sex with M., an ex
(not mine) of the late, great & much missed Percival
P. OR (example two) crime scene confusion – who
topped who & with what – transgender spillage (pillage)
a root cause?
                        That pause, Jesus, was much needed –
Tuesday now, sex my limit, voice culled, cute
commercials sold for a song.

Friends Gone & Friends Still Here

This weeping, Wilbur, it got to stop.
Sam, much appreciated if you could stop leaving, even
    for one day, your dead at my door.
Charles, I reckon your hate crimes are cute & certainly
    à la mode, but once again you've forgotten to wear
    the Dog for Sale sandwich board when you went
    to the corner shop for milk.
Dreadnaught days, Doug, were what we had, & we
    shoulda kept 'em.
Kick off those blue suede shoes, Sheldon, they ain't
    got no soles anyway, & do a jig just for me.
I know who put that talking in you, Earl; it was that gadfly,
    Pearl of Jam.
I'll flush you out, Frank, with a fire hose/a water cannon,
    whatever it takes.
Carl, if you had even an ounce of courage you'd
    come out of that commode & face the music.
Jake, admit you'd take commission, or communion,
    whichever came first, from anything that moves.
Harry, is jumping through hoops all you can do?
Never again will I be slop in your bucket, Bob, no siree.
My apology, Angus, I couldn't comprehend how much
    of a mere slip of a boy you were.
Kept supple by a haint, Harold, what a gas
    that must have been.
Close call, Calvin, you almost got delivered by rote.
Of your many mothers, Marvin, of wig, pump, knot,
    puzzle & plank, which one weaned you?
Repent, Rob, 'fore your bloodline makes a beeline to
    a Bob's-your-uncle unctioning.
Here's one for the road, Ron, your last.

Acknowledgements

Some of the poems in this book first appeared in the following journals: *Above Ground Testing* (Canada), *Azul* (Holland*)*, *Broadkill Review* (USA), *Cordite, Famous Reporter, foami:e, Great Works* (UK), *Green Dragon* (South Africa), , *H/EAR, Hobo, Imago, Jacket, Jossour, LiNQ, Mascara, Meanjin, Melaleuca, New England Review, Otis Rush, Overland, papertiger, Phoenix Review, Poetry Australia, Poetry International Web, Poetry Monash, P76, Razor, Sidewalk, Southerly, Syllable, Thylazine* and *Unlikely Stories* (USA)

and in the following anthologies: *AU/UA* (Ukraine), *La Traductiere* (France), *Light on Don Bank, Spineless Wonders, The Argument from Desire, The Best Australian Poetry 2008, The Best of the Ear, The Indigo Book of Australian Prose Poems, The New Australian Poetry, The Noise of Exchange, The Penguin Anthology of Australian Poetry, The Penguin Book of Modern Australian Poetry* and *25 poetes australiens* (France).